WITHDRAWN

ALPHONSE BERTILLON

(Comme a dit Molière) Il avait le repart brusque et l'accueil loup-garou, et mauvais caractère inimaginable.

EDMOND LOCARD

C'est là l'opinion d'un ami qui le tenait en très haute estime et qui a voué a sa mémoire un véritable culte en rendant en toute occasion un hommage enthousiaste et vibrant non seulement à l'intelligence du savant mais aux qualités morales de l'homme privé.

SUZANNE BERTILLON

ALPHONSE BERTILLON
A photograph taken by his pupil R. A. Reiss.

Alphonse Bertillon

Father of Scientific Detection

by

HENRY T. F. RHODES

*With Eleven Plates in
Half-tone*

GREENWOOD PRESS, PUBLISHERS
NEW YORK

ACKNOWLEDGMENTS

ALTHOUGH this book appears under the name of one author alone, it could not have been written without the assistance of collaborators whose co-operation it is a privilege to acknowledge.

First must be mentioned the relatives of Alphonse Bertillon, all of whom have given invaluable help. They are Mlle Suzanne Bertillon, Maître Jacqueline Bertillon, and Dr François Bertillon.

For a reason which appears in the text much of the Bertillon correspondence has not survived; but I have had the great advantage of learning from his relatives—who as young people knew him well—as much as, and perhaps more than, the lost correspondence would have disclosed. This applies, in particular, to Mlle Suzanne Bertillon. She was in close touch with him during his last days. Most of the surviving correspondence I have read was supplied by her, as well as the family photographs. She also kindly lent me a number of technical books and papers, now long out of print and practically unobtainable. Mlle Suzanne Bertillon is the author of an important book published in Paris in 1940—*Vie d'Alphonse Bertillon*. It is a book which should be read by every student of Bertillon's life.

From Maître Jacqueline Bertillon and from Dr François Bertillon I have also had great help in connexion with documents and personal information.

Secondly, I have had from Dr Edmond Locard, formerly the distinguished Director of the Laboratories of Technical Police at Lyon, help with technical and personal facts without which it would have been impossible to write this book. As a young man, Dr Locard was a pupil of Bertillon, and, as a person, he knew him well. He understands, perhaps better than anyone living, the relation between Bertillon's personal and scientific life. This relation must be the focus of any attempt to appreciate the real nature of Bertillon's achievement.

Dr Locard is also one of the greatest living authorities on the Dreyfus case. Most of the technical information, both published and unpublished, upon which the account in this book is founded originated with him. In this connexion it would be less than fair not to add that in his opinion Esterhazy was, in fact, the author of the *bordereau*. As shall be found, my own view is that, while the innocence of Dreyfus is beyond dispute, there is not conclusive evidence concerning the authorship of the document on account of which he suffered so much.

There is, of course, a considerable literature which any student of Bertillon's life and work must consult. The help I have received from these sources is acknowledged in the list of references.

H. T. F. R.

CONTENTS

PART ONE
The Questing Beasts

PART TWO
The Life

PART THREE
The Work

PART FOUR

Post hoc sed propter hoc

APPENDICES

ILLUSTRATIONS

PART ONE

THE QUESTING BEASTS

1. THE DISTILLER OF WINE

ON a morning in July 1912 the police of Chambéry, in France, were at work on the scene of a murder and robbery which had been committed in a small house on the outskirts of the town.

Two women had been stabbed, and the police were searching for clues which might confirm suspicions they had as to the authors of the crime. With them was a man whose clothes and bearing seemed out of place amid the blood and disorder found in the room. Chairs had been overturned, a bottle lay on the floor near one of the bodies. On the table was another bottle and four dirty glasses with dregs of wine in them.

The man's height alone made him stand out from the rest. He was well and strongly built. The features were good, but the face was haggard and the eyes deep-set. Most incongruous of all were his clothes—he wore an immaculate frock-coat.

His name was Alphonse Bertillon, Chief of the Department of Judicial Identity of the Paris Prefecture, and it would perhaps have been impossible to find throughout the French Police Force anyone who looked less like a crime investigator. The one thing which seemed to connect him with the unpleasantness in the disordered room was the fact that he was examining the bottles and the glasses with a lens. Before touching them, he had taken a handkerchief from his pocket, which he used to prevent leaving his fingermarks upon the surface of the glass.

The slow, methodical way in which he worked and the great precautions he took in handling everything he examined used to try the patience of some of the detectives and police with whom he co-operated. As late as 1912 the supreme value of fingerprints and other scientific evidence was not fully appreciated even by the higher ranks. Tact was not among

Bertillon's virtues. He used to complain that the police had
no appreciation of the significance of small clues, and he used
irony and sarcasm to make his point. Bertillon had little use
for detective stories except to barb his shafts; but if he thought
that some important article found on the scene of a crime had
been carelessly handled or improperly packed he had been
known to quote some appropriate saying of Conan Doyle's
famous amateur sleuth: "Oh, how simple it would all have
been if I had been here before they came like a herd of
buffalo, and wallowed all over it!"

The police of Chambéry and elsewhere probably reacted
no more kindly to remarks of this kind than did the fabulous
Inspector Lestrade. None the less, they had learnt from experience that Bertillon helped them to solve many problems. In
this particular case they were in some difficulty. Two men,
named Passieux and Girard, had been arrested upon strong
suspicion. They said they were innocent of both robbery and
murder, and the evidence against them was not complete.

Bertillon's minute examination was coming to an end. He
put away his lens. The police surgeon was examining the
bodies of the victims. One of the assistants began to pack the
bottles and glasses in ingenious little wooden crates, so constructed that the surface of the glass was protected from
chafing which might destroy the fingerprint or other evidence.
Bertillon turned his back sharply on the medical work in
progress. Experience had not blunted his dislike of the sight
of death by violence.

"There is nothing more for me to do here, Inspector. But
you say you have two suspects already. I must fingerprint
them."

"Very good, sir. I hope you have found something useful
to us?"

This incautious approach was greeted with a cold and
hostile stare.

"How can I answer that question? I am Chief of the
Identity Service, not a magician. I don't know."

The Inspector took no more conversational risks as they
drove to the station, where Passieux and Girard were under
lock and key. Bertillon and his assistants produced their finger-

printing apparatus. Printing-ink was carefully spread upon a highly polished steel plate. The finger-ends of the suspected men, pressed upon the inked surface, were then transferred to pieces of white card. They left with the sets of Passieux and Girard's ten fingerprints.

It was in his photographic room or his laboratory that Bertillon was most at home. He liked to write long and detailed reports. In this one he speaks of the photography of these fingerprints. Those on the bottles and glasses were photographed under the laboratory arc-lamps. The specimens taken from the fingers of the suspected men were also photographed and enlarged to exactly the same size, so that every detail could be seen clearly.

On the first bottle there were three fingerprints; on the second, four. On the four glasses two clear prints were found upon the second and fourth. The marks upon the first and third were smudges only.

These were Bertillon's words:

. . . We can conclude with absolute certainty that the impressions A, B, C, D, K, and M [six of the prints found on the bottles] were made by the suspect Peter Passieux.

In regard to Girard, our considered opinion is that the impressions E, F, G, and L [the prints found on the glasses] are his, but we have found only a minimum number of points of resemblance, so that corroborative evidence is required to establish conclusively his presence on the scene of the crime.

This is one of the cases which gave Bertillon his reputation as the first fingerprint man. He was not entitled to this distinction, and, as shall be found, he made no such claim himself. His true fame rests upon a different achievement which is none the less solid. There are other means of distinguishing one man or woman from another besides the method of comparison of their fingerprints. Bertillon was the first to devise one. It was recognized throughout the world to be a great discovery, because it converted the traditional business of identification into a systematic method founded upon scientific principles. The old methods had been mere guesswork, and they were the cause of many miscarriages of justice.

This does not make Bertillon's work with fingerprints less

significant. He had a particular genius for investigating problems concerning fingerprints, and most other matters relating to crime, which others had overlooked. But even in his day-to-day work, his careful research with lens and camera throws light upon the character of the man, reflects his history, and mirrors events which took place long before he was born. He was not the first of the family to be a " questing beast."

His grandfather, Jean-Baptiste Bertillon, was born at Dijon in 1785. After serving in Bonaparte's army, he had become a chemist-distiller in Paris. At a time when laboratory work was not thought as important as it is now he was devoted to experiment. Jean-Baptiste did much to improve the distillation process, but his most important chemical discovery was a method of purifying sugar which is still in use to-day.

Having no commercial flair, he was lucky enough to have married Pierrette Garinot in 1820. She was a diminutive person with a shrewd business head. While she never made her husband a rich man, she took over the counting-house, where she felt as much at home as he did in the laboratory. There was, however, more to her character than a commercial sense. Pierrette Bertillon could share her husband's intellectual life and interests. Proof of her own survive in books she read and highly prized—miniature and finely printed editions from Rabelais to Voltaire. She read voraciously by candle-light after the busy days were over.

Incidentally, Pierrette Bertillon helped to bring the reign of candle-light to an end. Her husband was still a schoolboy when Murdock was making his experiments in Birmingham to see if he could light the city with gas. Paris did not follow suit until 1833, but Bertillon was associated with the first gas-works, erected some years before in Paris, and he retained an interest in it until the end of his life. As with his other ventures, it was the experimental work and the chemistry of the process which were his contributions. He had nothing to do with the distribution of that then particularly evil-smelling mixture. That this new piece of research and development added substantially to his income was no accident. Behind the scenes was his shrewd, diminutive wife controlling the financial reins.

MEMBERS OF BERTILLON'S FAMILY

(*Top left*) Georges, his younger brother; (*top right*) Achille
Guillard, his grandfather; (*bottom left*) Jacques, his elder
brother; (*bottom right*) Louis-Adolphe, his father.

14

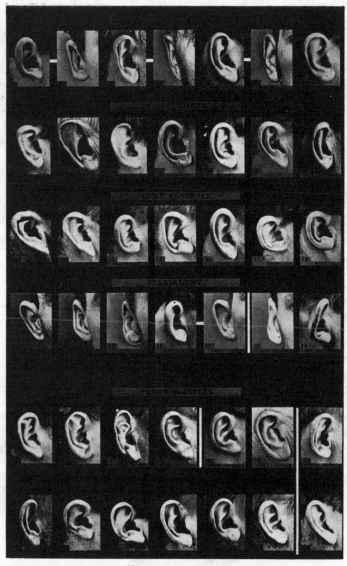

"Look at his Ears!"

An example of Bertillon's sectional photography, which is the
basis of the *portrait parlé*.

[*See pp.* 104–105.]

Long before this Pierrette Bertillon had contrived so to conserve the family resources that there was enough to buy a small house in Paris and a little estate called Le Buisson, on the edge of the Montargis Forest. It is a pity that she did not live to read her Rabelais and Voltaire by gas-light. She was taken by the scourge of cholera which, first sweeping London, reached Paris in 1832.

It was a heavy blow to Jean-Baptiste and to his son, Louis-Adolphe, who was then a boy of eleven years old. One of the more remote results of the death of the wife and mother whom both loved was a breach between father and son.

The reason for this will presently appear. Louis-Adolphe Bertillon was the father of the strange and contradictory creature who is the subject of this book. A little of the adventurous story of his early years must also be told, because it throws light upon the life and work of the son. Alphonse Bertillon did not gain renown by accident. It was, so to say, in the family. Jean-Baptiste, his grandfather, was not interested in crime or criminals; he had never heard of anthropology or fingerprints. No one knew of them in his time. But we have observed his curiosity and his love of experiment as a means of ferreting out the truth. Louis-Adolphe Bertillon shared his father's ignorance of criminals and fingerprints, but we shall see him experimenting just as his father did. But in his case the world was his laboratory and men and women his experimental material. The same was true of Alphonse—except that his world happened to be the world of crime, although his discoveries had a universal influence far beyond it.

2. THE ANGELIC DOCTOR

QUEEN VICTORIA was seventy-eight when, at her command, the British Ambassador decorated Alphonse Bertillon for his work in connexion with the wreck of the *Drummond Castle*. She was twenty-one when his father, Louis-Adolphe Bertillon, became a first-year student of medicine at the Sorbonne.

The year 1840 was a stirring time. Britain and France were at odds concerning Egypt, Suez, and Syria. Admiral Stopford, supported by Austrian and Turkish ships, appeared off the Syrian coast. Beirut was bombarded. Thiers made a bellicose speech in the Chamber which annoyed Louis-Philippe. Napoleon's ashes were brought from St Helena to Les Invalides. The House of Orléans was sitting upon the volcano which was to erupt in 1848.

Something of more immediate interest to a young medical student was a famous murder-trial which also took place in that year. Louis-Adolphe was a student of Orfila's laboratory, and he probably saw the great medico-legist demonstrate the newly discovered Marsh Test for arsenic which has been the turning-point of so many notorious murder-trials since.

Marie Lafarge was accused of murdering her husband by poisoning him with arsenic. There was a battle between the experts. His professor appeared for the Prosecution, and the brilliant but less well qualified Raspail for the Defence. Orfila, solid and imperturbable, proved that there was a lethal quantity of arsenic in Lafarge's body. Raspail created a sensation with the ingenious theory that the victim had been poisoned by the arsenic-laden atmosphere of the town of Glandier, where he lived. Although found guilty, Marie Lafarge was later pardoned. The affair is one of the great mysteries of the history of crime. There really was a grave doubt concerning the facts.

Louis-Adolphe had quarrelled with his father over the choice of a career. Because he was himself devoted to research, Jean-Baptiste wanted his son to study commerce so that he could take over the financial side of his business. He obstinately resisted his son's first choice of engineering as a profession. But the son could be obstinate too, and he set his face against commerce. Finally there was a grudging compromise whereby, oddly enough, the father accepted the alternative of a medical course. But he was not fully appeased, and he refused to give his son an adequate allowance.

Louis-Adolphe's life as a student was thus a hard one. Precisely where he lived is not known, but it must have been near the 'Boul Mich,' and probably in one of those narrow and still not too clean streets hard by Saint-Germain-des-Prés. He had one room where he ate, read, and slept.

Because of the shortage of money, as much as by taste, he was a recluse who read more intensively than many students, and not only physiology, anatomy, and medicine. One of the books which aroused his enthusiasm was Quételet's *Social Physics*, the first classic study of the natural history of man in terms of measurement and arithmetic. It was an exciting discovery to learn that measurements of the human body revealed statistical laws, showed that no two human beings were exactly alike, and that these propositions could be proved by collecting facts and figures. That measurement was the basis of the study appealed to the engineer he had once wished to be, as well as to the student of physiology and anatomy he now was.

There was a career in this. Louis-Adolphe did not wish to be a practising physician. He wanted to make his mark in some new field of research. Social physics seemed to point the way to it.

Although he did not know it, the tide of social events was carrying him in the same direction. The political situation had deteriorated. One of the symptoms of it was that the lectures of the great historian Michelet were shaking the College of France. He was a brilliant demagogue, and did not mince his words. It was 1844. Michelet had recently published *Priests, Women, and Families* and *The People*.

Louis-Philippe and the Clerical Party were not amused. The reaction of the Party was hostile and violent. They tried to secure the suspension of his course at the College.

The students thronged Michelet's lectures, and Louis-Adolphe was among them. No one knows what his political opinions were at that time, but he always had the Frenchman's traditional suspicion of politicians. By instinct he was a Liberal and a Republican, like most of his fellows in the medical school and scientific faculties.

They believed in the principles of liberty, equality, and fraternity, and wanted to show their loyalty to a respected professor who believed in the same things. Retiring and modest though he was, it was Louis-Adolphe who suggested that a medal should be struck in Michelet's honour. It was voted unanimously. He collected the subscriptions, had the medal made, and organized the whole conspiracy. Because of the circumstances, they all thought it must be discreetly done. Not even the professor was to be informed of the presentation until the last minute. To his embarrassment, Louis-Adolphe was chosen to make the presentation and the speech.

It did not work out quite according to plan. On the day agreed upon the professor was unexpectedly absent from the College. More and more apprehensive as the time approached, the young man was glad of the respite.

It was not to last for long. At seven o'clock next morning Louis-Adolphe was in bed. It was winter and cold. Not being able to afford the luxury of a fire all day, he was under as many blankets as he had. There was a loud knock on the door.

He got up and hastily put on an overcoat over a night-shirt due for the laundress. He had never mixed in politics, but in such times it might be the police.

The shock was even greater when he opened the door. Professor Michelet stood on the landing. An unhappy undergraduate flushed and stammered, acutely conscious of a room unaired and in disorder. On the table there was even an unwashed coffee-cup from the night before.

" May I come in, Bertillon? Important business!"

" Yes, sir, of course! But I am afraid the room——"

The professor gave one of his booming laughs.

" Even professors of the College of France were students once, you know." He looked doubtfully at a decrepit chair, but decided to sit down. He was a heavy man.

" Now, what have you young fellows been up to? I understand you are the chief conspirator."

" We wanted to make a small presentation, sir. We were going to—we didn't know you knew anything about it."

Michelet laughed again. " These things leak out. I keep my ear to the ground. I have to. Now that the secret is out let us arrange it. What about the day after to-morrow? "

Louis-Adolphe no longer felt embarrassed at the thought of his speech.

" I shall look forward to it, sir."

" So shall I. You are a medical student, aren't you? "

" Yes, sir."

" Good. It is a pleasure to me that as many medical and science students attend my lectures as history men. History is a science, not an exact one, but a science. It is my business to try and teach people that. We shall meet the day after to-morrow."

They were to meet many times. Doctor and historian were close friends until Michelet's death. But it was not his influence which was decisive in moulding the young doctor's career. A year or so later he was to see by chance the notice of a course of lectures by a Dr Achille Guillard on demography.

He was diminutive, like his mother. The first thing that struck him was the lecturer's height. He stood six feet, and he had a massive black beard. His manner was in strong contrast to Michelet's. Without eloquence or gestures, the quiet voice vibrated through the room. Louis-Adolphe did not then know precisely what demography was, and it was significant to find that it was the scientific study of regional groups and races. Guillard knew how to enlarge the context to show how this study could produce a better society and a new order of man.

" I should like to meet Dr Guillard." He said this to a fellow-student who attended with him.

" He is very approachable, they say."

" It seems like that from the numbers. I don't like pushing myself forward."

" You will get your chance."

Louis-Adolphe was indeed to get his chance, although not quite in the circumstances he expected. In the meantime, the lectures urged him to a serious study of anthropology. He was a newly qualified doctor with a precarious living to make. With his taste for engineering, it was fascinating to design instruments to measure body and limbs accurately, although he could not yet afford to have them made. The budding research-worker had to content himself with existing measurement statistics and with the simpler ones, such as the heights of university students from different parts of France, which he could compile himself.

When, as shall be seen, his son Alphonse Bertillon gave his report to a sceptical Prefect of Police concerning the identification of criminals he illustrated his arguments with graphs which the work of his father had inspired. Quételet studied the heights and chest measurements of army recruits. He discovered that there was an average size to which the majority of about seventy per cent. approximated, with some fifteen per cent. on each side of that average who were either larger

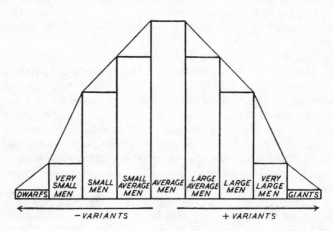

FIG. 1

or smaller (Fig. 1). Of course, it was known before that giants and dwarfs are rare, and those of average size numerous. What Quételet discovered was that the variations were in conformity with certain mathematical ideas of Newton and Gauss.

In this human context this graph has been called Quételet's curve. Louis-Adolphe Bertillon carried the discovery a stage further with the work he began about 1846. Using the same methods of measurement, he showed how the results could be applied to distinguish one race from another. When he grouped the measurements of the heights of the inhabitants of the Department of Doubs together they did not conform to Quételet's curve. It rose, fell, and then rose again (Fig. 2):

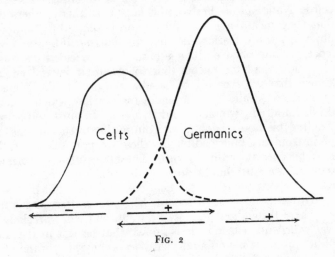

Fig. 2

This was because there were two sets of averages. If the lines were completed at the point of the trough two curves were produced, both of Quételet's shape. These corresponded to two types of men in that region, one with a tall and one with a much shorter average.

Without this pioneer work, there would have been no system of criminal anthropometry, the first method of identifying habitual criminals, with which began a new era in crime investigation.

3. REVOLUTIONARY INTERLUDE

HOWEVER much Louis-Adolphe may have wished to avoid politics, no man can ignore a revolution.

On February 3, 1848, Paris awoke to the ominous crackle of musketry, which had not been heard in the city for eighteen years. He heard the shouts of "Vive la Réforme!" "Vive la Garde Nationale!" Perhaps he hoped, as many others did, that they meant a better future for France. But, although physically quite fearless, he thought that bloodshed and violence accomplished nothing useful. What decided his course of action were the events that followed. It is well enough known that the shooting of a subaltern outside the Ministry of Foreign Affairs was the signal for a volley which brought down hundreds, wounded and dying, in the dust and smoke.

After this Louis-Adolphe was out in the streets with his case of instruments, unarmed but for these weapons of mercy. He took no special credit for this. The ethics of his profession required that he should do what he could for the wounded and the dying whatever political colour they might be.

With characteristic reticence, he seldom afterwards spoke of where throughout the city he went, and what precisely he was called upon to do. It is known that he was in the thick of it. He must have found plenty to occupy him in the black days of June, when, in the Red rising, the Archbishop of Paris was murdered and ten thousand men were killed and wounded in a pitched battle with the troops under Lamoricière.

As a reward, he was thrown into prison. No one knows upon what charge—if upon any at all—he was arrested with many hundreds of others when an armed and uneasy truce settled upon the city. One of the complaints made against the old order by advocates of liberty of thought and conscience was the activities of a corrupt and tyrannical secret police force. They wanted to see it abolished. But the new régime not only took over the old political police machinery —it improved upon it. When this Second Empire ingloriously fell there was not one secret police force, but half a dozen. This explains how many decent and law-abiding people were imprisoned upon the slenderest evidence or none at all. Louis-Adolphe was a scientific man and thus traditionally suspect in any case. He had committed the crime of helping both sides without trying to distinguish sheep from goats when it was impossible for an honest man to do so. He was probably under suspicion as an 'intellectual' and therefore at best as a dangerous anarchist in humanitarian disguise.

The Sainte-Pélagie Prison whither he was taken by an armed guard had not improved since Appert, the prison reformer, had reported upon it in 1836. Indeed, it was probably worse, with a higher percentage than usual of the Parisian population under lock and key. It was crowded with new arrivals, and smelt of stale urine and bodies not recently washed. The place was full of filth and noise.

In the room where he was locked up, the motley groups, if not actively hostile, received him without enthusiasm. The room was already overcrowded. But suddenly his bewildered and depressed spirits rose. There was a face he knew. The height, the massive black beard, and—even here—the carefully tended hair were unmistakable.

"Monsieur Guillard! You may not remember me. I attended your lectures."

The bearded man looked at him closely.

"I remember. It's Bertillon, isn't it?"

"Yes, monsieur."

"What are you here for?"

"I don't know," said the young man truthfully. "I wish I did."

"I know. I know very well; but we can't discuss that here." He drew Bertillon aside, and spoke in a low voice. "There is at least one police agent in every room. But I have friends dealing with this. The first thing is to get better lodged."

And better lodged they very soon were, by the standards of Sainte-Pélagie. Louis-Adolphe was afterwards to look back

upon this unexpected and trying interlude, and to find a good
deal on the credit side. At least their common mischance had
thrown him together with the man he most wanted to know.
Also Guillard, more mature and politically conscious, showed
no bewilderment at their predicament. In the long run he
thought the new Government might be less reactionary and
more sympathetic to liberal and scientific ideas, even if they
were still suspicious of them.

They lay in prison six months, but the time was not wasted.
It was here that the blue-print of the Society and School of
Anthropology was prepared. Guillard was enthusiastic. The
school must not only teach anthropology, but must bring
together all the vital sciences, and show how statistical methods
could be applied to every kind of scientific work.

With the great advance of the science of anthropology in
the twentieth century, this is not news to-day; but it was a
new concept in the middle of the nineteenth century. It is a
study in contrast to look back and realize that two of the men
who began this great advance in knowledge did so when in
prison.

For the result of their initiative was the formation of the
Society and School of Anthropology. Louis-Adolphe was one
of its vice-presidents. The internationally renowned surgeon
and anthropologist, Broca, was its secretary until his death. In
a few years it became a scientific and intellectual centre known
throughout Europe.

With so much in common (including adversity) it was
inevitable that the friendship of these two men should ripen.
When they were released Bertillon was received and accepted
by the Guillard family as a matter of course. He passed with
honours the shrewd examination of Agarit, Guillard's wife,
and a hard-headed daughter of a ribbon manufacturer of
Lyon. She was at the same time fully attuned to the intellectual climate her husband enjoyed.

There was a family of nine, and among them Zoé Guillard,
the best-looking and most elegant of a good-looking family.
Although he used to complain of her extravagance, she was
closer to her father than the rest, and shared his tastes and
interests. This was uncommon among young women at that

time, but the Guillards were people who did not conform to the conventional pattern. From the first, Louis-Adolphe wanted to make Zoé Guillard his wife. On account of his diminutive size and scholarly habits, he was shy of women. Not, it seems, of her, for an understanding soon arose between them. This was the woman whom he married in 1850.

PART TWO

THE LIFE

4. THE BIRTH OF ALPHONSE BERTILLON

IT was April 24, 1853, and one of those soft, luke-warm days with muted sunshine spreading over the city of Paris which always makes spring there the most satisfying of miracles. After the hatreds and bloodshed of the Revolution of '48, and in spite of the man-made tensions following it, Nature seemed to promise, as a good spring always can, a better and a brighter future.

But if Nature was calm and peaceful outside in the Rue de Rivoli things were not the same inside No. 22. There a new baby, not long born, had been making that April morning hideous. He was not at that time very much to look at. This latest Bertillon specimen was under-weight, and his colour was not all that it should be. But there was energy within the meagre frame, for the creature howled and howled as if in protest at the very fact of being born.

Despite the noise and disorganization of routine which any birth must produce, even in the best-regulated household, Dr Louis-Adolphe Bertillon was looking at his second son with pride. If his expression was tinged with anxiety this was due only to the vague fear of anything which disturbed the programme of the research worker, and forced him to face a new concrete situation. None the less, however distasteful, he could deal with that aspect of the matter. One of the things which made Louis-Adolphe Bertillon the distinguished father of a son who was to become more distinguished still was that in his mind and heart scientific abstraction and practical social responsibility achieved a definite, if sometimes a precarious, balance. All his adult life through he had been, and he still remained, an excellent and conscientious physician. He had personally attended his wife, whom he dearly loved. She had not had too difficult a labour and delivery, and was in good health and spirits.

With a last look at his son, whose protests became, if anything, more furious, Dr Bertillon went into the next room where his wife lay in bed. He bent over and kissed her. Zoé Bertillon smiled.

" We will call him," she said, " Alfred. I have always liked that name."

" Very well, my dear. Alfred it shall be. I must go and register it."

Dr Bertillon passed into the Rivoli, turning towards Sebastopol, which was the direction of the nearest *mairie* where the registration could be made. In honour of the occasion he wore his top hat and his black cloak. The good physician liked to affect the costume of a horseman, so that he also wore high boots. Most sensitive concerning his height, he imagined, quite wrongly, that high boots gave an illusion of extra length to legs which were disproportionately short for a short body. He walked as usual with his head lowered and with hands clasped behind his back. Now he had forgotten his pride in the newborn son; he was oblivious of the soft air of spring and of the breaking blossom of the lime-trees in the Tuileries. He was, in fact, probably thinking about toadstools—being at that time devoted to mycology—and deep in the problem of how to classify *Agaricus* or *Boletus*. He arrived suddenly, and, as it seemed to him, inexplicably, at the *mairie* door.

The man who, without batting an eyelid, had gone unarmed into the streets under a hail of bullets in '48 to tend the wounded and dying, irrespective of which side they served, and who had been cast into prison for his pains, was known and respected by every one in the 2nd *arrondissement*—and far beyond it, for that matter.

" Good morning, doctor."

" Good morning. Ah, yes, of course. It is a question of a son."

" My congratulations, doctor. The registration clerk has no one with him just now. Please come this way."

" My congratulations," echoed the clerk. " And to madame! They do well, I hope?"

" Excellently; but he makes a good deal of noise. It is a little trying."

" Ah, a boy! They do, sir—they do indeed." He lifted a quill pen and dipped it into a large inkpot filled with the log-wood ink beloved by French officials even to this day. " And the name, doctor? "

Dr Bertillon looked at his inquisitor as if he had asked him some abstruse medical question, unanswerable without notice —if answerable at all.

" The name!" he said. " Of course, the name—it is most provoking, but it has slipped my memory. Now, let me see— it began, I am sure it began, with an A."

The clerk, with pen poised, smiled encouragingly.

" Alexandre, perhaps? "

" No, too ambitious."

" Alcibiade? "

Dr Bertillon was exasperated perhaps less with this new suggestion than at his own lapse.

" Alcibiade," he said, " Alcibiade—perfectly ridiculous."

The clerk drew himself up slightly. " I beg your pardon, doctor. I was only trying to be helpful."

" My dear fellow, you must excuse *me*." Suddenly his face cleared. " And you have helped me. It began with Al— Al . . . Alphonse! It must be Alphonse."

The pen came down to the paper. There was a methodical scratching . . . Bertillon. Alphonse, born April 24, 1853. " And the religion of the parents, doctor? We have to add that."

" None."

The pen traced the word in the appropriate column, the writer allowing himself an almost imperceptible sigh. He did not share the doctor's free-thinking.

Elated that his memory for routine detail had not, at long last, played him false, Dr Bertillon returned to his house. It was now full of people. From every point of the Parisian compass grandparents, uncles, and aunts had come to see the newly born Bertillon. The proud father announced the news that little Alphonse was now a legal citizen of France.

" Alphonse!" said his wife. " But we said it was to be Alfred!"

Neither the Bertillons nor Guillards were a family to make heavy weather over trifles. Every one laughed at the doctor's consternation.

"I must go and put it right at once."

"No," said Zoé Bertillon; "it is well enough as it is. I like Alphonse too. I refuse to make you, as a statistician, confess to those form-fillers that you have made a mistake about your own son's name."

"It is ridiculous that my memory should mislead me like that—and disappoint you."

"It might have happened to anyone. We have a good deal to think about."

It would not have happened to Zoé Bertillon. She was a Lyonese, who, like the Yorkshire folk, have hard heads and soft hearts. The attractive, elegant exterior and the soft voice concealed a strong realism, which her newly born son was to inherit. Coming from an academic family, she also had intellectual capacity, which her scholarly husband could, and did, respect. She loved music, sculpture, and books, and she had advanced social ideas at a period when such things were thought scarcely decent in a woman.

It was this that she and all the Bertillon circle had ' to think about' at that time. In the France of the '50's it was almost as dangerous to be a 'progressive' as it is in America to-day. Neither Bertillon nor his father-in-law Guillard was ever actively involved in politics, but this did not save them from the suspicion of being fellow-travellers with dangerous and bloodthirsty anarchists. Their crime really was that they were the pioneers of the scientific revolution which was sweeping Europe, and to which France had made such brilliant contributions, and particularly in the application of scientific methods to the study of mankind and society. This approach alarmed, to the verge of panic, all political and ecclesiastical orthodoxy whatever its label. In the light of this it can be understood how so great a Humanist as the historian Michelet —who belonged to the Bertillon circle—should have been deprived of everything, short of his actual liberty, as if he were a dangerous revolutionary. The scientific spirit itself was suspect, precisely because it saw, or thought it saw, through the glass of scientific laws and order the vision of a new society better and more just than the old.

It was this sort of tension which drove the Bertillon family to Montmorency to escape the political police of Paris. At the time, perhaps on the very day, that Alphonse was born the doctor had been warned by his father-in-law that it would be prudent to leave Paris since he feared another scientific witch-hunt. Practising what he preached, Dr Guillard prepared to leave himself, and it was fortunate that he did so. Shortly after his departure his house was surrounded by armed men who had been sent to apprehend him. Dr Bertillon had already acquired a practice in Montmorency from an old physician who wished to retire. With the practice went a pleasant house. The family was installed there in August 1853.

It is an ill wind which blows no one any good. The change of *milieu* probably saved Alphonse Bertillon's life. He was extremely fragile and sickly, and, although suffering from no specific disease, his health was a constant source of anxiety to his parents. At Montmorency there was good fresh air. The house was spacious, with a large and excellent garden. It was the air and the garden which brought Alphonse back to life. If he did not become as robust as his brother Jacques, two years his senior, his health improved; he put on weight more rapidly and began to crawl and then to walk no later than other children.

It has been said of him that as soon as he could speak his scientific education began. In 1854 Dr Guillard, his grand-father, had published his book on human statistics, entitled *Démographie Comparée*. His father was passionately inter-ested in it. Dr Bertillon remained loyal to his toadstools, but he believed that the statistical methods whereby his father-in-law classified and individualized human beings could equally be applied to the classification of plants. There were long sessions in the garden of Montmorency when the young and middle-aged savants discussed the implications and possibilities of a science which had been unknown until the nineteenth century, and which they were among the first to exploit. Literally they were giving pattern and shape to Napoleon's inspired guess when he said, " La statistique, c'est le budget des choses, et, sans budget, point de salut public." It required a new language, which the children, playing in the garden, overheard, and which, if it had no precise meaning for them then, had a stirring sound. Perhaps it is not surprising that almost as soon as he could speak the young Alphonse was one day heard to remark: "Demography, it is my grandfather who invented that."

In after-years both Alphonse and his brother Jacques often confessed to looking back to those three years at Montmorency with an intense nostalgia. Perhaps the children owed more to Montmorency than they knew. For all the Bertillons, adults and children, it was a tower of ivory and a garden enclosed against a troubled world. In the case of Alphonse at least, it may have been much more than that. Who shall say to what extent the imprint of the then mysterious words of a new science upon the young subconscious may later have inspired him to turn that science to a new and vital social use?

5. EDUCATION OF A GENIUS

IN 1856 the Bertillons sold the house at Montmorency and returned to Paris, where they rented an apartment, No. 14 Rue de Bruxelles. Dr Bertillon and his father-in-law were deep in their statistical investigations. His room was full of calipers and gauges used for anatomical measurement. Even at the age of three, these mysterious instruments fascinated Alphonse and his elder brother. It was the beginning of an education in the guise of an intriguing game. In the course of a month or two they had measured with pieces of ribbon every article of furniture in the house.

There were many friends. Zoé Bertillon would not allow her husband to become over-absorbed in his chosen subject. The Countess d'Agoult, friend of Liszt, was among them, and von Bülow the musician, first husband of Cosima Liszt. Whatever interest he may have found in them as persons, Dr Bertillon had none in their music. He was absolutely tone-deaf. Alphonse inherited this defect.

But scientific men preponderated in the distinguished company. There were at least a score who were devoted to the statistical techniques of Bertillon and Guillard, and who foresaw a great future in the statistical approach to the sciences. Among them was the biologist Letourneau, who was strangely fascinated by phrenology, which he insisted was a legitimate branch of scientific knowledge.

His diagnosis of the Alphonsean bumps, upon which he begged to be allowed to make a report, was not borne out by the facts at that time, although it was later to be spectacularly vindicated. He said that Alphonse had a precise and orderly mind and a strong taste for mathematics.

The evidence seemed to be all the other way. In 1859 Jacques, the elder brother, entered the Imperial Lycée Bonaparte, now called Condorcet. Alphonse would have remained at home for the time being, but he proved so rebellious and undisciplined that his parents decided that he must go to school. He was accordingly sent to the Chaptal College.

Alphonse Bertillon was not there long. He was entirely unmanageable. Not only was he the despair of his masters, but his rebellious spirit infected his fellows. After one term the principal insisted that he must be removed from the school.

The boy's health may have contributed to his pugnacious and anti-social attitude. He was at this time very big for his age, but he was anæmic and highly strung, and he suffered periodically from intense migraine which would yield to no remedy. His worried parents decided that he must be educated at home.

The choice of a tutor was not a fortunate one. It fell upon a young German student, timid, shy, and extremely short-sighted, one of those individuals whom cruel circumstance will sometimes single out for a life of martyrdom at the hands of ill-conditioned little boys. By being expelled from his first school, Alphonse had achieved his end, which was to avoid being taught or disciplined in any way. It would take more than a short-sighted German tutor to defeat him.

At the first lesson it was not difficult to possess himself of the young man's spectacles and to place them upon his own nose. Quite blind without them, the unfortunate tutor searched every inch of the floor upon his hands and knees with his nose glued to the carpet. Failing to find them, more time was wasted in an attempt to read his pupil's abominable writing with the naked eye. It was no more difficult to replace the lost spectacles on the table than it had been to secure them in the first place.

A bolder manœuvre was to disappear into a cupboard while the tutor was absorbed in the impossible task of deciphering and correcting the Bertillon exercise books. As soon as the door had closed upon the disconcerted and nervous young man who had gone in search of him the pupil emerged to sit at his table and await his tutor's return with an exasperated father. . . .

" I have been here all the time. When he takes his glasses off his sight is so bad that he couldn't see me. I am very sorry for him, but it isn't my fault."

Dr Bertillon did not believe this obvious falsehood, but he was too impatient to inquire into the matter, and he thought the tutor a fool.

The farce continued for some months. Periodically the tutor lost his glasses and his pupil. During instruction in history (fanatically hated) ill-drawn caricatures of the kings of France mysteriously appeared dangling from strings. To the short-sighted and harassed tutor they seemed to float crazily in mid-air without visible means of support.

It has not been recorded whether the unfortunate young man, at his wits' end, resigned or whether he was dismissed by his exasperated employer. The matter is of no importance. As a result Alphonse achieved his aim, which was in no circumstance to undertake scholastic work of any kind.

Allowance had still to be made for his bad health. This was a reality of which, none the less, he knew how to take advantage. His talent for making himself unbearable, which had been reserved for his masters and tutors, was now turned upon the household. Having exasperated his brother and harassed the servants, he could retire to his chaise-longue and write to his aunt : " Ne faisent rien, mais rien, ce qui s'appelle rien."

There was more in this than met the eye. Behind the temperament and the tantrums there was a brain at work. In the summer of 1863 the Bertillons took a house at Saint-Valery-en-Caux. Zoé Bertillon wanted to rest on the beach and to read the ethics of Spinoza. The Michelets were with them, and the great historian laughed when he heard Madame Bertillon's choice of holiday reading. Progressive though he was, he could not believe that women understood philosophy.

It was Zoé Bertillon who laughed last. In a few days the professor of history was to be found continually upon the beach arguing the merits of the systems of Comte and Spinoza with the young and elegant woman, the wife of his disciple.

If Zoé Bertillon surprised Michelet it was as nothing to her surprise when she read the letters which Jacques and Alphonse

exchanged at this time. Jacques was a slow-working but steady
scholar and inclined a little to superiority because of his hardly
won progress. He describes the new methods of classification
of rare plants (the Latin names are all quoted) which his
grandfather was studying in Italy. Included in this category
were pineapples (*Ananassa sativa*) and hemp-seeds (*Cannabis
sativa*). Not to be outdone, Alphonse retorted with grandiloquent descriptions of the marine plants he was collecting on
the sea-shore.

There was some mockery in this, but behind was a real preoccupation with the Latin and the botany and the need to
label the things they handled if they were to be recognized
and understood. It was a precocious correspondence for boys
of eleven and thirteen, and it has a strong flavour of exhibi-
tionism not uncommon at that age; but at least it was related
functionally to what they were to achieve thereafter.

But the holidays came to an end, and with their conclusion
returned the perennial problem of what was to be done with
Alphonse. The school had been a catastrophe; the tutor a
disaster. A boarding-school seemed to be the last resort. There
existed at this time in Charleville, Ardennes, a school known
as the Rossat Institution which was considered satisfactory for
' difficult ' children.

It has been said by a distinguished mathematician that most
teachers, if honest, would admit that children would get on
quite as well in class if the teacher were not there at all.
Whether we think this rather sweeping statement is true in
general or not, it undoubtedly applies to a certain number of
children, of which Alphonse Bertillon was certainly one. For
the truth is that he is an outstanding example of one of those
' problem types ' who could and did acquire knowledge in
spite, and not because of, those who lamentably failed to drive
it into him.

This notion would not have found favour in French educa-
tional circles in the middle of the nineteenth century—even at
Rossat, which accounted itself a modern school. Alphonse
Bertillon lasted the usual term. The inevitable letter arrived.
A much tried principal wrote that he would not " at any
price " retain this good-for-nothing pupil.

A vivid portrait has been drawn of the boy, thirteen years
old, by his niece, Suzanne Bertillon:

> He was a big boy, but slim to thinness, pale-complexioned
> with arms too long and shoulders too wide. But it was a hand-
> some face framed by dark chestnut hair which curled close
> against the head. He had grey eyes with mockery in them.
> With his fine sense of the ridiculous which he could exploit
> for amusement's sake, he liked to play to the gallery at the
> expense of the stalls. But he had also a temperament which
> could be sad and black and intensely irritable. It concealed
> an acute sensitiveness and a fear of showing his feelings.

It may seem odd at first sight that such a creature should
aspire to be a man of science, but this was his instinctive
means of compensation even at that age. When he returned
for the second time in disgrace it was to argue his case with a
long-suffering parent whose sensitive pride was wounded. Dr
Bertillon had all the virtues and shortcomings of an agnostic
saint. Before all things dedicated to his work, anything which
distracted him from it was a kind of sacrilege. This prodigal
son, whom he loved in his remote fashion, was distracting
him.

"You are impossible, Alphonse. Jacques gets on well at
school and work. Little Georges learns to read and write. You
learn nothing."

He saw at once that the prodigal was penitent, however
short-lived that penitence might be, and that he was unhappy.

"I learnt botany and natural history—and swimming,"
said Alphonse. "They interest me. I can't see the use of the
Latin verbs and the French grammar."

The doctor recalled the scarifying report. Its adverse com-
ments, concerning Latin and French grammar and the rest,
had not embraced botany and natural history. He knew they
were taught and made a mental note of what might be a
significant omission. But he must make all his points.

"The principal also says that you are inattentive and that
your manners are insupportable."

"Well, they were always saying in class, 'Scholar Bertillon,
you are not attending. Repeat the last thing I said.'"

" And what did you say? "

" That terrestrial earthquakes cannot deflect the stars from their courses."

" What? " said his disconcerted parent.

" Of course, I knew he hadn't really said that, Papa; but I had to answer, and I said the first thing that came into my head."

Dr Bertillon, that gentle, remote man, never acted on the spur of the moment. He was the reverse of anything which is understood by the term ' heavy father ' at a period when heavy fathers were the rule; but, if persuasive, he was determined in his fashion in the last resort.

" Listen, Alphonse. Botany and natural history are very good things. They are part of my subject, but at your age you have to learn other things. I had to. There are examinations, and the *baccalauréat*. You have to start with that."

The boy did not answer the challenge directly.

" Papa, please don't send me to boarding-school again. I want to be at home and see you and Grandpapa work. It's real work, not like school at all."

How many mid-nineteenth-century fathers would have appreciated this? Even this modernized specimen saw his queer, precocious son through a glass darkly; but at least he knew that here was a being it was not safe to drive, and a very unhappy one at that. He did not allow his words to match his thought.

" It depends very much on you. Your behaviour is out-rageous. You don't seem to fit in even here. Go and think over what I have said."

Dr Bertillon had a good deal to think over himself. Into what kind of hole could this queer-shaped peg be made to fit when the day-school, the tutor, and boarding-establishment run on modern lines had failed to produce the necessary pattern? The only light upon a dark horizon was the botany and natural history. And Alphonse read. He had once sur-prised him with a copy of Quételet's *Physique Sociale*. It seemed strange reading for a boy of thirteen, but this at least portended a serious interest. Because of the letters Alphonse wrote and his passion for collecting and arranging his natural-history exhibits, his botany seemed to promise something more than an ephemeral school-boy hobby could promise.

The doctor sighed and took refuge in Letourneau's diagnosis of his troublesome son's bumps, indicating a brain devoted to precision and order. He thought phrenology absurd, but hoped that his young colleague might be right, even if for all the wrong reasons.

The problem remained unsolved. In any case, it was soon to be thrust into the background by a more serious disaster.

6. ZOÉ BERTILLON

The good die first,
And they whose hearts are dry as summer dust
Burn to the socket.

Wordsworth

THE early and mid-nineteenth century tended to gloat a little over early death, and with some reason. The truth was that the good, and the bad for that matter, often died sooner than they should. Twenty or more years later Bertillon was to welcome Louis Pasteur to his department as a visitor. Had the initiator of bacteriology been born at the beginning of the nineteenth century instead of at the beginning of the third decade of it, Zoé Bertillon's life might possibly have been saved.

As things were, she lay on her death-bed in May 1866, being not then thirty-five. Neither the doctor nor any of his colleagues seemed to have gained the slightest clue as to the nature of her illness. It was certainly some gross bacterial infection, beginning with a slight fatigue and a temperature which rose suddenly and alarmingly, bringing delirium with it. The temperature could not be brought down, and the best that could be done was to use such means as were then known to relieve the overstrained heart and lungs.

It was to no purpose. After three days she was dying. She sent for her children, as the custom then was. Jacques, Alphonse, and even the little Georges were there.

Characteristically Alphonse shed no tears. He looked at his mother with a set face; but a heavy thud shook the floor almost exactly at the moment that she breathed her last. Alphonse had fainted—it was an hour before he came to.

His family might nickname him " the barbarian," but his

mother had never subscribed to that. Without spoiling him
or petting him in any way, she had always treated him as if
he were a human being. He was no problem to her.

The boy repaid this with a devotion which was none the
less deep that no show need be made of it. His mother did not
occupy herself with him overmuch. She was a great reader
of sociology and actively concerned with a group of young
Parisian women who interested themselves in education, for
the sake of both knowledge and citizenship. They were
regarded as progressive and even dangerously so. Perhaps the
secret of her influence over her son had been that she laughed
at his tantrums and refused to take seriously his sinister record
at school. She never lectured the boy or expressed any
anxiety as to his future, and she never used his nickname of
"barbarian." Without intruding upon his private thoughts,
she established a closer contact with him than any other member of the family.

They used to walk in the Tuileries. Without constraint he
would tell her how much he hated school and how much more
he learnt from books than from the masters who tried to teach
him, and why it was that botany and natural history were so
much more important than Latin grammar. How much his
mother really appreciated what was even then fomenting in
that turbulent mind we do not know. What is certain is that,
without making a parade of it, she loved this strange, good-
looking creature who quarrelled with every one and who
treated those in authority in barbarian fashion according to
the standards of an authoritarian period.

The bond which united them was perhaps that both mother
and son were people of the future. Zoé Bertillon conformed
to no conventional standard of her period. Intellectual
interests among women were just tolerated, although frowned
upon; but in France, as in England, to be respectable, they
must be associated with the 'blue stocking.' Strange though
it appears to us now, a woman who displayed interest in things
of the mind and in elegant clothes at the same time could
incur the suspicion of being no better than she should be.
When these things were combined with scepticism in theological matters the case was so much the worse. The un-

pleasant scene with the Bishop of Orléans when this charming
and much loved woman came to be laid to rest on May 31,
1866, is a significant sidelight upon the contemporary attitude.
When he heard that the ceremony was to be a civil one the
bishop wrote an episcopal charge concerning the scandal and
social dangers of burial without benefit of clergy. He sent
this charge to her husband. The gentle doctor was not to be
intimidated by an indignant bishop.

> I do not wish to give offence, much less to scandalize any-
> one. But my wife was a liberal and had ceased to believe in
> the Catholic faith. The scandal would have been if I had
> allowed her to be buried with religious ceremonies she did not
> believe in.

This rebuke, if anything so moderate can be called that,
had all the more force because Louis-Adolphe Bertillon spoke
for his dead wife rather than in defence of any act of his. He
knew she shared his integrity and honesty. Alphonse shared
those qualities too, but at that time they were not unassuming
at all. If he was a barbarian it was because he thought it
right, if he spoke at all, to say exactly what he meant, regard-
less of the consequences.

He had his honesty from her as much as from his father,
but at the beginning of his romantic education she had found
the means to smooth away its sharp and obtrusive corners.
When the family complained of his temperament and bad
manners Zoé Bertillon always rose in defence of her black
lamb. He was good-looking in his Byronic fashion (they could
not deny this) and charming, if one were tactful.

And this was also true. Being at ease with her, he dropped
the mask of the sardonic style and the pose of the *enfant
terrible*, and even began for her sake to respect the gifts of
charm and elegance which she carried so naturally. He
remained reserved and remote, but he ceased to be uncouth.

After the catastrophe of her death neither the father, the
husband, nor the sons of Zoé Bertillon displayed any of the
conventional pomp of mourning. Always something of a
recluse, the doctor withdrew still further and buried himself
in his work. The first effect upon the lonely son was to leave

him practically isolated and in fierce and inarticulate revolt against a fate which had so suddenly struck down the thing he loved.

They went that summer to Ussat-les-Bains, leaving Jacques behind at his boarding-school. Although Alphonse did not know it, this was a sentimental journey for his father—*une recherche du temps perdu*. His father and mother had spent many holidays there in the first years of their marriage. Dr Bertillon said nothing of this. Thermal treatments, he said, interested him, so that he had arranged to be appointed medical director of the establishment at Ussat. The appointment was a minor one, and it interfered with his research work in Paris. The truth was that he wanted to escape and to leave the recent memories of Paris behind.

His opinion of the establishment and his work there is an index of his social attitude at that time. He wrote to his older son: " There are three companies exploiting the waters here, and they compete fiercely with each other. This does not make for efficiency. On the contrary the treatment suffers. There is no co-operation."

But what was lost on the swings was gained on the roundabouts. It was there that the friendship between father and son began which lasted throughout the father's life. Hoping to recall the ghost of the dead, perhaps Dr Bertillon discovered, in the place he had hallowed, that it lived in his children.

He began seriously to concern himself with his son's aversion from learning. They wrestled together with the problems of French syntax and Latin and Greek verbs. He was surprised to find Alphonse more receptive and persevering than he had expected. If this were encouraging, his interest in more advanced studies was more so, even if it introduced the old difficulties that the boy wanted to run before he could walk. In the quiet of this retreat by the side of the Ariège, most beautiful of mountain rivers in France, Dr Bertillon's medical duties left him time for editorial work upon the *Encyclopædic Dictionary of Medicine,* that classical book which is still in current use in France under the title of *Le Dictionaire Dechambre.* Included in it were, of course, the researches in vital statistics and demography to which Bertillon and Guillard were devoted. If Alphonse was still shy of Latin and Greek there was no doubt about his enthusiasm for the " demography his grandfather had invented " and for his father's anthropology. He had that sharp appreciation of the visual which made him the lover of curves and graphs, even if their significance was not fully understood. He listened and asked questions—very much to the point for a boy of not yet fourteen.

It is not difficult to reconstruct the picture of the scientific scholar and the melancholy, difficult, and yet eager son poring over the charts and figures, with nothing to disturb them in that quiet house above the river except the hiss and swish of Ariège as it ran down to meet Garonne at Toulouse. The death of the woman both had profoundly loved had forged a new affective link between them. Louis-Adolphe Bertillon would have recognized no difference in the quality of his love for his wife, his friends, and for his work. Through her death, there was that amount of the affective drive left over to apply to vital statistics, humanism, and science.

Secretly, the same process was inarticulately at work in the son. In his case, of course, the unexpected enthusiasm for work was a more direct compensation for adolescent sorrows. But, whatever the immediate cause, the result was solid enough. Apart from the formal education whereat his father seemed to be succeeding where two schools had ignominiously failed, he would not have neglected the field work if he could have found it. Alphonse writes to his young brother Georges : " There are no mushrooms and no insects here, so that I don't know how to occupy myself when I go out walking."

There were compensations for these disappointments. If Alphonse ever walked with Reclus, who came by chance to Ussat for the season, he could not have complained of being without occupation on those excursions. Reclus, the most brilliant geographer that France or perhaps Europe has ever produced, was one of the most unconventional of Dr Bertillon's unconventional friends. In an age when such personalities have almost ceased to exist it is refreshing to recall a man who held as a matter of principle that, whatever Government there was, he was ' agin it,' who was a convinced anarchist and food- and dress-reformer, and who was so genuinely contemptuous of money that—despite his professional distinction and prestige—he was always in the most acute financial difficulties. Such scientific Bohemians are now an extinct species.

Dr Bertillon, before all things a liberal, had a great sympathy with anarchism, although he rejected it in political theory and practice; nor did he believe in the food-reform and the long clothing for men, and the sandals. There were long and stimulating discussions. What the doctor did believe in was his friend's vast erudition and his firm grasp of and imaginative approach to the problems of geography, a subject which both higher and lower schools generally managed to deprive of all vitality.

And Alphonse listened. He was a good listener when interested. Of all the subjects they had tried to hammer into him at his two schools he had most obstinately rejected geography. The Reclus version of it seemed to be a very different thing. This may explain how it came about that the only book he ever wrote closely touches upon a subject which schoolmasters had somehow first taught him to hate. There is no conclusive evidence, but it seems highly probable that Reclus was the first inspiration of *Les Races Sauvages*, which Bertillon published in 1882.

The Ussat season was coming to an end and with it the doctor's duties as medical superintendent of the clinic. They must inevitably return to Paris and to family responsibilities, made heavy by the death of the mistress of the household. Like an incubus they lay upon the doctor's soul. The diligence taking them northward to Toulouse bumped and rattled. . . . Jacques must continue at the Lycée Bonaparte; Georges must go to a preparatory school. . . . Ah! Foix. There was the castle on its high crag beyond the town. Alphonse was looking moodily out of the window as they crossed the bridge. Beneath, the Ariège, much wider now, swept on. Dr Bertillon gave his son an apprehensive glance. What about Alphonse? He must go to school.

Dr Bertillon had noticed that ever since his son walked with his mother in the Tuileries in her last days he had become very neat and careful with his clothes. He was even oddly dandified in a sober fashion. The Imperial Lycée at Versailles!

It was a good school, and they wore a smart uniform. He might like that.

II

Alphonse liked the dark-blue uniform with gold buttons well enough, and while the novelty remained his anxious father received reports encouraging an optimism which was to be short-lived. Schoolmasters were his son's natural enemies, and they repaid his war of attrition with despatches which became increasingly critical and depressing in tone. Had he known it Dr Bertillon might have found grains of comfort in the fact that there were exceptions among the hated race. The reports were uniformly bad, but in fact Alphonse made some progress in mathematics quite simply because the man who taught loved his subject. Perhaps it is better understood to-day than it was then that there are many children who can learn only for pleasure and can win knowledge only from those who teach for it. The example here is the unknown 'modern' who wrestled with the problem of the Bertillon mathematics. He really loved his profession. Sensing disinterested enthusiasm, as boys will, Alphonse gave him very different value for his scholastic money.

If his form-master, who taught him most subjects, had understood the problem as well as the mathematician the reports might have been better. He was a small man with a bald head, a moustache carefully waxed, and powerful glasses set upon an aggressive nose. He was the slave of routine technique which he thought infallible. It included the device of restoring attention by demanding a repetition of the last word spoken, and the customary sarcasm at the pupil's impudent and irrelevant reply. There were a hundred lines for Alphonse, and as an addition to the sentence he was to be kept in on Sunday.

The theologians fared no better; and it was, in fact, in the divinity class that a major crisis occurred. It was the worse that Alphonse excelled in divinity. His verbal memory was good, and he had long passages of the Bible by heart. His father had insisted that he should be taught according to the Protestant faith. The pastor was a dull and long-winded pedant, fair game for the unregenerate little monsters who without sign or word spoken somehow formulated a conspiracy to make the unhappy pastor's life a burden. By an instinctive process of selection Alphonse became the ringleader of it. . . .

" The woman whom thou gavest to be with me, she gave me of the tree, and I did eat."

The Bertillon voice, pitched so as to be just audible, addressed a neighbour.

" I never liked apples. I will never eat one again."

" Silence, Bertillon, and pay attention."

The next move in the campaign was for some one to ask a seemingly innocent question, seeking enlightenment upon some obscure point. Whatever the answer was, it was Bertillon's cue to refute it with the help of long passages from Holy Writ.

It is not surprising that the reports became more and more querulously outspoken. Dr Bertillon went to Versailles to interview an unimaginative but much tried headmaster. His remarks were even less encouraging than his writings and more brief—" *Tenue mauvaise, conduite mauvaise, caractère difficile.*"

For once Dr Bertillon lost his temper. There was a terrible scene in which Alphonse was threatened with immediate withdrawal from school and employment in any capacity where strict discipline would be enforced. Under duress the boy was made to write a letter to his father promising amendment. This document, dated March 29, 1869, has been preserved. Even the hour at which it was written, 2 o'clock, is superscribed. It contains promises of amendment worth perhaps less than the paper on which they are written.

Nevertheless, the summer term passed at least without very outrageous incident. The boy disliked Versailles, but disliked still more the alternative of a more remote boarding-school or work as a *saute-ruisseau*.

And he was to engineer an artistic revenge in the holidays. July came and with it the end of the term, a fever, a temperature, and a sore throat. His father was alarmed, for the boy's general health was still subnormal, and even minor ailments he thought should be treated seriously. Alphonse was kept in bed. Jacques, his brother, perhaps a little arrogantly fresh from passing his *baccalauréat* in science, thought he was making the most of it, as, indeed, perhaps he was. He wrote thus to a cousin :

> . . . His room makes one think of Aunt Mary's. There are two tables one on each side of his bed laden with basins, syrups, purgatives, emetics, and tonics which I am sure Papa never ordered him to take. . . . And he has besides water bottles, napkins, and astringents which he uses to gargle with as noisily as he can. . . . He has a fire in his room at this time of the year—and all for a slight sore throat.

It would be interesting to know to what extent these youthful temperamental disorders were the reaction of a sensitive personality to the disorders and conflicts of the social background. There is no more vivid description of it than a letter he wrote himself during the holidays which they joyfully took that year at Vascoeuil when Alphonse had recovered from an illness which his father took seriously even if his brother did not. Reclus, the wandering geographer, came and went mysteriously at midnight and dawn. The Michelets were there. Alphonse read Pascal, to whom he remained devoted all his life, and went for long solitary walks in an enflamed anti-Republican countryside. In a letter to his family he describes how at Coutances some thirty peasants, armed with old rifles and rusty sabres, calling him a Republican and " Parisian dog," placed him under an escort of six with loaded rifles to take him to the *gendarmerie*. There he angrily claimed police protection and got it. He found accommodation and a bed while the crowd demonstrated outside against Republicans who came to set fire to the village and with infernal machines to blow them all up. A baton charge dispersed them.

The boy who could make such heavy weather of a temperature and a sore throat clearly knew very well how to take care of himself and seemed quite unalarmed by the experience.

" But I was glad," he said coolly, " to get back to Vascoeuil next day with all my four limbs."

This was how it had been, and particularly for Liberals and Republicans, ever since the revolution of '48, five years before Alphonse Bertillon was born. To-day we have the mass murder of modern war, or the threat of it, subconsciously to disturb the emotional lives of our children, but perhaps the grave social tensions of France of the mid-nineteenth century may have produced the same effects. Added to it, the rising generation was to have a foretaste of what bigger and better wars were to be like, for the catastrophe of '70 was rapidly approaching. It was not for nothing that Bismarck had said that it was the business of victors to leave the vanquished with nothing but eyes to cry with.

It was also the time of Alphonse Bertillon's last and most inglorious term at Versailles. He was expelled for behaviour— in the opinion of the authorities—so outrageous that nothing could extenuate it. Theoretically they had reached the higher flights in classics, geography, modern languages, and the rest. Alphonse systematically idled, but the demon which is in most schoolboys was soon to find work for idle head and hands to do. He had developed an interest in cooking and spent the time which should have been occupied with Thucydides in devising an ingenious method whereby his culinary experiments could be conducted in class. The capacious desk common to French schools at that time concealed a spirit lamp, chocolate, and a miniature saucepan. The utilization of a dozen eggshells carefully chipped to form miniature cups has almost a touch of genius. They were small, light, and could be immediately disposed of in the event of an alarm. With this equipment chocolate, thick and hot, was regularly distributed to eleven companions who were so fortunate as to sit near enough to Alphonse Bertillon.

It might, but for an unlucky accident, have continued the whole term: a fire broke out one day, and all attempts to extinguish it were unavailing. However tightly the desk-lid was held down dark smoke and a nauseating stench of burning chocolate rose in the air. Even the absent-minded and irritable classical master immediately detected it. Calling loudly for water, he advanced upon the burning kitchen and its cook, who still vainly strove to compress smoke and flame. He was ordered to retire, but remained still gripping the desk-lid. The angry master attempted force. A heavy book lay on the desk. Perhaps rejoicing in a kind of desperation that he could at last find a use for a Greek dictionary, Alphonse suddenly rose and hit his enemy over the head with it. It was a shrewd and well-timed blow which felled the alarmed and exasperated classicist.

The rest was cries, confusion, and pails of water. With them arrived the Principal of the Imperial Lycée of Versailles. What immediately transpired at the subsequent interview is not known, but a letter arrived for Dr Bertillon next day requesting him to remove his son from the school.

July 19, 1870, came with its disaster for France and finally put an end to Bertillon's scholastic career. He was separated from his father and brothers, first at Caen and then at the Lycée in Havre, which did nothing to close the gaps of a neglected education. His father, remaining in Paris, became mayor of the 5th Arrondissement. Reacting typically, the scholarly recluse embraced energetically the responsibilities he instinctively shrank from. He organized with exemplary efficiency the distribution of such food as there was to a cold, hungry, and almost desperate population. Louis-Adolphe Bertillon is one outstanding but typical example of that fortitude and absolutely selfless devotion which the people of France develop and know so well how to utilize in times of crisis.

With such an educational background, at eighteen years of age it seemed that Alphonse Bertillon's scholastic record must be written off as a total loss. But at twenty he surprised every one by passing his *baccalauréat*, although without distinction, in science and literature. Perhaps it will never be known by what process he achieved this educational success, mediocre though it was. It was some balm to his father's wounded pride. In spite of his liberal convictions, prescribed courses of study and orthodox examinations were articles in Dr Bertillon's creed. To ignore the one and fail in the other was a disgrace. In fact, he had himself and his father-in-law to thank for his son's lately won and unspectacular success. When the young man had returned to Paris after the war with characteristics and a habit of mind which seemed to point to a good-for-nothing future his grandfather, Dr Guillard, had taken him in hand. The now ageing professor had lost his wife. He had himself retired; but for solace in his affliction Dr Guillard had returned to his first enthusiasm of teaching the young. He was one of those rare preceptors to the manner born who could arouse the conviction in the pupil that there was no such thing as a truth (as Aristotle said) which was a truth for nothing. In consequence everything he taught was informed and illuminated with a kind of meaning which Alphonse Bertillon had never grasped or thought important at school. His scholastic success, such as it was, stemmed from the things he absorbed on his own initiative and from his father and grandfather.

7. ENGLAND

THE relieved satisfaction with which the Bertillon family greeted what they thought to be new signs of grace in the black sheep was short-lived. Dr Bertillon was now once more in despair. Alphonse showed no inclination to follow up his scholastic success. His burst of energy came to an end, and he would settle to nothing. He became more moody and temperamental than ever.

At his wits' end, Dr Bertillon secured a post for him as a junior clerk in a bank. No details remain concerning this disastrous interlude. The only qualification he could conceivably have had was the neat and correct appearance which he affected and which was in such odd contrast to his undisciplined character at that time. At least he looked the part.

It is quite certain that his behaviour did not match the correctness of his clothes. If his letters written at that time were typical of his calligraphy this alone must have sorely tried superiors, who, above all, demanded a "good commercial hand." It is not difficult to imagine the consternation of the chief cashier when he saw the hieroglyphics with which the bank books must have been decorated.

If Alphonse Bertillon survived a month of this servitude it would be surprising. There was a family conference to decide what was to be done in this extremity.

It used to be said in England that a fool must be sent into the church. The custom in France was to deal with difficult cases in a last resort by sending them to England, "where at least they would learn English."

Alphonse Bertillon accepted this decision with satisfaction. At cross purposes with his family, and unable to adjust himself, it was a means of escape.

Severe shock though this exile was in some ways to prove,

it was the real beginning of his education. Where he lived
when he first arrived in London is not certain, but it may have
been No. 54 St Mary's Terrace, Paddington, where he
afterwards lodged. Hard by is the still dignified Paddington
Green with its fine plane-trees and its statue of Mrs Siddons.
He would have appreciated that because of its slightly Parisian
flavour. Bertillon's views upon ecclesiastical architecture are
not known. His æsthetic taste was never highly developed if
it existed at all; but it would be interesting to know what he
thought of St Mary's, Paddington, that eighteenth-century
box-like monstrosity, with its pseudo-classical decor, which
still stands at the corner of the street in which he lodged.
No. 54 has gone, replaced by a block of flats, but some
interesting examples of early nineteenth-century terrace houses
remain, similar to those which once filled the terrace. They
are in decay, but show melancholy traces of the dignity they
must have had in the '70's.   ·

It was January 1874. London, and Paddington in particular, may not have been looking its best. His letters home
complain of the fog and dampness. But the matter which
throws most light upon his reactions to a foreign land is the
curiosity with which Londoners in bus and railway carriage
seemed to regard him. Alphonse Bertillon was a sensitive
young man, and, although he never complained that the
curiosity was offensive, it embarrassed him, and the more
because he did not understand the cause. A French acquaint-
ance, with more experience of London, enlightened him.

" It's your clothes," he said.

This was to touch Alphonse Bertillon in a sensitive spot.

" My clothes are all right," he said indignantly.

" Of course they are all right. You look very chic. There
isn't really so much difference between French and English
clothes, but there are the details and the way to wear them. I
like the English, but they have the oddest prejudices and they
notice these things. Of course you know they call us frogs."

" Yes, of course."

" But did you know that many of them really believe that
we live on them? That is why they call us that."

" What!" said Bertillon. " You are not serious." He gave

one of those shouts of laughter which always surprised those who did not know him well, and who thought he seemed lacking in a sense of humour.

" I am perfectly serious. It is very singular."

This conversation worried the young man. A law unto himself in major matters, he was extremely correct as to dress and deportment. He began anxiously to study his fellow men, to change the style of his hair and to make such alterations in his dress as he could. His father's refusal to send him money to make the necessary changes in his wardrobe was a severe shock. It was an unsympathetic letter. Not only was additional money refused, but he was told that his allowance would be discontinued, and that he must find means of supporting himself. For all his patience, Dr Bertillon, like his father before him, was not incapable of severity. He evidently thought the time had come for this problem child to learn his lesson the hard way.

It was severe enough as it turned out. Reacting energetically in the face of an unpleasant prospect, Alphonse, with hardly enough English to keep body and soul together, yet managed to become registered with two or three employment agencies specializing in the supply of not very well-paid masters to teach in private schools. By this means he arrived some time in February in Smethwick, to take up his duties as professor of French at the Collegiate School, under the headmastership of William Grant, A.C.P.

His letters concerning the scholastic life, shrewd and penetrating, depict the pedagogue as a type rather than an individual. Mr Grant survives the analysis better than many of that period might have done. Alphonse Bertillon was miserably paid. There were many economies bordering upon the parsimonious, but at least the austerities were not applied at the exclusive expense of the pupils. Mr Grant had some pretensions to professional competence and some notion of his responsibilities as a teacher of the young.

There were dramatic interludes. When Bertillon first arrived to teach French at Smethwick he was almost without a word of English. His method of instruction, improvised on the spot, was to write down on the blackboard an elementary

French vocabulary and against it the English equivalents hastily but laboriously looked up in a dictionary. It was the kind of opportunity at which he would have rejoiced as a schoolboy himself, and his English scholars did not hesitate to take advantage of it. He was obliged to turn his back upon the class to write on the board. This was the signal for a number of audible remarks and titters. Although he did not understand the words he rightly interpreted them as personal and uncomplimentary. Alphonse Bertillon turned sharply and just soon enough to observe a rapid concealment of pea-shooters. Something must be done at once if his prestige was not to be wrecked. From his own record he knew that there was always a ringleader : he had been one in his time. He spotted the boy at once and advanced towards him, demanding by signs the delivery of· weapon and ammunition.

The boy stood his ground, and when his French professor was close enough spat at him. Had Bertillon had the means to deal with this critical situation with suitable words of command and reprimand he might have used them. But he was restricted to gesture. The one he chose was, rather naturally, to box the young man's ears.

There was pandemonium. He caught the words Frenchman and Englishman, and realized that racial instincts had been stirred. The ringleader, with two or three of the bolder spirits, was advancing. Amid the hubbub he waited for them behind a chair, ready to strike a blow not only on his own account, but for France. Fortunately for scholastic decorum, the door at that moment suddenly opened and the Principal entered the classroom.

He quelled the rebels with a cold and glassy stare. There was a dead silence. Mr Grant had no French. He looked interrogatively at the now flushed and embarrassed professor of French.

His gestures more than sufficed. Bertillon pointed at the ringleader and then at his jacket soiled with spittle.

" Thompson," said Mr Grant, " come here."

Reluctantly but without hesitation, the miscreant came forward. Mr Grant made a sign which the Frenchman did not understand. The boy bent down to receive immediately six to a dozen strokes from a resilient cane which Mr Grant drew from the folds of his gown.

Corporal punishment has always been unknown in France. This swift and painful retribution must have taken the young Frenchman aback, and it may have shocked him. What followed amazed him still more; but it wedded Bertillon to England for ever. He did not follow what headmaster said to boy, but he understood what followed. These were, in fact, the words, or words to that effect.

"And now, Thompson, go and shake hands with M. Bertillon and apologize."

The boy advanced. Although obviously smarting severely from this practised application of the cane, he showed no resentment. Thompson even smiled. He looked at his hand, perhaps to decide if its cleanliness would pass muster, and nervously shook hands with Bertillon, muttering embarrassed but clearly conciliatory words. Instinctively the young Frenchman realized that it was not the cane alone or fear of it which had induced the change of heart, but that he had done the right thing in boxing that boy's ears and standing his ground thereafter. The ringleader and the class not only bore him no resentment, but respected him as a person to be reckoned with.

He had no further serious trouble with his French class, except that, for the most part, they seem to have learnt no French. Writing to his brother, he says they had three years' instruction in the language and then had hardly thirty words. There were one or two who took French a little more seriously. When his English had improved Bertillon suggested to his principal that French in the form of a little literature and history might encourage the more enthusiastic students. Mr Grant agreed, but his reaction to the suggestion that they might begin with Voltaire's Charles XII opened Bertillon's eyes to yet another inexplicable facet of the English character:

"Voltaire, M. Bertillon, not Voltaire if you please. We do not approve of, or even mention, that author in England."

The boys took no interest in languages, because all of them wanted to become chemists. He thought this was the irresistible force of circumstances, because Smethwick was ringed with chemical and metallurgical works, and the fathers of a number of the scholars were themselves chemists or the managers or directors of these factories. Smethwick was like a great crucible reeking with the fumes which these boys liked to reproduce in the laboratory.

English women hardly disconcerted him less. He writes to his father in February 1874 concerning his *" maîtresse "* *(d'anglais)* :

> Having been a mistress in an English school at Chantilly, she speaks French well and has helped me greatly with my English. She is *très aimable . . . fort jolie . . . très polie.* But like them all full of virtue and modesty and cotton next the skin [*coton sur la poitrine*].

When Mr Grant came to write Bertillon's reference he had "pleasure in stating that he has discharged his duties satisfactorily and that his character has been unexceptionable." By this ambiguous phrase perhaps he meant that, as French characters go, it might have been worse. A man who thought the works of Voltaire unmentionable might have worded his reference differently if he had read the letter above.

The reference is dated June 17, when Bertillon gave up his teaching work at Smethwick. Mr Grant gave as his reason that he had "an insufficient number of pupils to keep him employed." In fact, it is likely enough that Alphonse Bertillon, justifiably dissatisfied with his salary, had asked for more and that since an increase was refused he decided to leave. It is not known by what means he made contact with the Hanbury family, of Strathgarve House, Dingwall, Ross-shire; but at that time he wrote urgently to France for a reference from a Protestant minister, upon which the prospective employers apparently insisted.

Here was a grave problem. The proper person to supply this reference was the theological master at the Lycée Imperial, who, as they were to discover, had not forgotten young Bertillon's near-blasphemous record in his scriptural class. Dr Bertillon, an excellent diplomat, managed to induce his friend the Marchioness of Charnacé to intervene. This most charming and tactful of all the doctor's friends arranged an interview with Alphonse Bertillon's former theological tutor.

It was to no purpose. The pastor absolutely refused to supply a reference in favour of a brand he had failed to pluck from the burning. Madame de Charnacé wrote to the doctor in comic despair, saying that her feminine diplomacy, far from achieving the desired result, had produced a sermon on hell-fire.

The matter was settled by another friend, himself a Protestant minister, who from " general knowledge " [that convenient term] testified as to Alphonse Bertillon's theological respectability.

It was thus that he came to be the holiday tutor of the young Hanbury boys at Strathgarve House. There is no detailed record of his short stay with them, but it seems that he at once made a most favourable impression not only upon his two pupils but upon the family in general. Mr Charles Hanbury then lived at Strathgarve House, and he also had a seat in England—Belmont House, East Barnet. He was killed when hunting with the Warwickshire hounds in 1900. Mr Hanbury had four sons and four daughters, older than the boys. The youngest, Mrs Kemble, the last survivor of the family who could have known Bertillon, died in 1952 at the age of a hundred. The boys were named Harold, John, Basil, and David Theophilus. Harold, who died nine years later, was then twenty. John was thirteen, Basil and David a year and two years younger. Bertillon tutored only two of the boys, almost certainly John and Basil. Bertillon himself said that they treated him more as an elder brother than a tutor. They taught him English games and perhaps to ride to hounds. It was a completely harmonious and happy association which seems to give point to Shakespeare's shrewd observation concerning Franco-British relationships.

> If that you will France win,
> Then with Scotland first begin.

Despite the difference in climate, the Scottish mountains and rivers may have recalled the halcyon days at Ussat-les-Bains. He would have loved the Alt Graat, that burn one hundred feet deep rushing through the narrow gorge, and the explorations of the mountains behind. He read Sir Walter Scott.

It was not to continue for very long. In the late autumn he
had to return south, unsettled and without any clear design
for the future. But he had not abandoned the hope of a
scientific career. He wrote to his brother that now he could
speak English fairly well (*passablement*) an English University
course would be very attractive. He had thought of Oxford,
but it was impossibly expensive. Edinburgh might be more
practicable, because the fees were less and he could have found
occupation during the vacation to help the finance. If this
was by way of a hint to his family that they might supply the
means to make him a university student they did not take it.
The truth perhaps is that Dr Bertillon was not prepared to
invest anything in his recalcitrant son's career.

He found new lodgings in London at 7 Arundel Street,
Coventry Street, Haymarket, and then secured a post at the
Collegiate School, Bishops Stortford, for the autumn term of
1874. The headmaster was a certain George Wilks, a Master
of Arts. There are few details, but in his reference Mr Wilks
said of him that he was " gentlemanly in appearance and
manners, and I believe his morals also are good."

Apart from this encouraging afterthought, it was the kind
of reference which would have insured him a post in another
school of a similar kind. But perhaps it was as well that
military service recalled him to France at the beginning of
1875. He might otherwise have drifted on, to be exploited by
one small academy for the sons of gentleman after another,
with little profit to himself or his pupils. In fact, Alphonse
Bertillon owed much to his stay in England. His father's
medicine, however unpleasant, was salutary. He had been
obliged to fend for himself in a strange land and had gained
thereby a self-confidence not formerly natural to him. He had
scored not only a scholastic but social success with a Scottish
family of distinction, no mean achievement in one of his
temperament. Even if he did not then know it, the British
interlude had set his foot on the first rung of a career.

8. THE EXASPERATED CONSCRIPT

HE may have had the first inkling of the profound change which England had wrought in him from the family reactions when he found himself, on balance, with pleasure and relief, once more under the parental roof, now in the Rue Monsieur-le-Prince. One of the things to take him aback was the fact that they looked at him almost as the English had done when he first arrived in London, but, as it seemed to him, with a certain awe. To begin with he was so much bigger than they were. Alphonse Bertillon stood five foot ten, which was much above the average height of Frenchmen at that time. Both his father and Jacques were pygmies beside him. His father was five foot one, and his brother but an inch taller.

And without knowing or affecting it, he had absorbed something of the English style, a kind of expansiveness, which he had lacked altogether prior to his visit to England. He was better humoured, more civilized, and amiable. Also, he could hold his own better with them. They had never been in England and could speak no English, so that in one respect, at least, he could claim international connexions which even his father and grandfather Guillard, his only equal in physical size, could not boast of.

But, going back to the library, he saw there the solid continuity of the old life. There were the calipers and gauges which Broca and Guillard had designed, the demographic charts, the facts and figures, and the formidable manuscript of the *Encyclopædic Dictionary of Medicine*, which had grown in size.

With this stable picture before his eyes, he was called to very different duties when summoned to join the 139th regiment of infantry, then stationed at Roanne, some fifty miles from Clermont-Ferrand. England had been in certain respects a salutary discipline of a kind, but it is hardly possible to imagine an individual less suited to military routine, and less likely to profit by it, than Alphonse Bertillon. Since the Franco-Prussian War the discipline in the French army had become more severe. The officer commanding his battalion seems to have specialized in the organization of all kinds of fatigue-parties. Besides brushing out the barracks, peeling potatoes (at which he seems to have been particularly inexpert), and clearing the latrines, there were a dozen other apparently less necessary, but equally fatiguing, operations to carry out. Despite the discipline he so much hated, if his picture of the military instruction of the infantry was accurate it does not seem to have been very thorough or efficient. They had daily instruction in musketry, but their duties appear to have ended at 3 o'clock in the afternoon. At 8 o'clock they had to be back in barracks. Lights out—the lighting was entirely by candles —was at 10 o'clock.

But in military as in civil life Bertillon kept to his habits of sartorial smartness. He had not been long in the army before he found a fellow conscript who for a franc would clean his buttons and equipment. As a result of this satisfactory arrangement, he was the smartest recruit on parade.

Either because of his appearance, or the fact that he was clearly better educated than most of his fellows, he attracted the attention of his company commander. He was invited to dine not only with his captain but with the medical and other officers of the battalion. His report in a letter to his brother that they all strongly advised him not to become a student of Saint-Cyr but to remain in the ranks is a tribute to their good sense. They evidently perceived that his wish to become a student at the College was not due to any enthusiasm for the profession of arms but a means of escape from the potato-peeling and the latrines. He admits as much in the same letter: " C'est l'occupation de la vie la moins pénible, mais on peut bien dire la plus ridicule possible. . . ." Alphonse Bertillon would certainly never have made a good infantry officer.

It was fortunate for him that the army, which at least at that time gave little attention to such matters, should have decided that he was unlikely to make an efficient infantry man, but that in a clerical capacity he might be of some use. How long he served in the ranks before he became the secretary of the colonel of his battalion is not known. He certainly served in this capacity for a considerable period of his military service. The choice was probably a sound one and based upon his qualifications. Most of his fellows could read and write only with great difficulty, and some of them not at all.

Alphonse Bertillon was one of those people whose fortunes never quite followed the orthodox course, perhaps because he showed originality and initiative in escaping from situations which he disliked. The French army did not then offer, as modern armies do, educational facilities of which men of all ranks can take advantage. But, by means unknown to this day, he contrived to follow the course for the ' first medical' at the University of Clermont-Ferrand. Utterly bored with the army life, which left him with much time on his hands, he asked his brother to send him books. They are not specified in the correspondence which survives, but some at least must have been books of anatomy. It is possible, of course, that the medical officer of the battalion, who was himself interested in anthropology and who knew his father, Letourneau, and other men of note, may have interested himself in the young man's aspirations. His family also had close associations with the university. Claude-Achille Guillard, his great-grandfather, had once been rector there. These influences may well have made it possible for some special facilities to be granted to him, although his military duties would have made it impossible for him to follow the orthodox university course in the normal fashion.

Nor were his studies directed along the normal route. They took a form which was closely adapted to the work which was later to make him famous. He became devoted to and almost obsessed with a specialized problem. This was the dimensions of the human skeleton. By what means he gained access to sufficient material to make a metrical study of the 222 components which make up the human skeleton is not known. He was familiar with anthropological measuring-instruments from his early youth, and he had seen Broca, Letourneau, and his father and grandfather use them. This may thus have presented no major difficulty. But it would be interesting to know what his colonel thought of a recruit who had at first talked of entering Saint-Cyr and who had now switched his attention to the study of human bones, and how his secretarial duties were reconciled with this new enthusiasm.

It seems impossible that his research could have advanced beyond the preliminary stage, but he seems to have formed the conclusion even at that time that anatomical measurement might be made the basis of a technique whereby individual identity could be established. At that time perhaps this was of less importance to him in practice than the fact that he inevitably learnt by this original and unorthodox means a good deal of anatomy and physiology. It seems improbable that a thesis, however original, which dealt exclusively with the method whereby the bony structure could be precisely measured would have been much help to him in passing a university examination for the ' first medical'; but he sat for that examination and he passed it with distinction. This was, in fact, his only systematic application (if it can be called that) to higher studies, the only gesture of acknowledgment he ever made to the formal processes of education by which his father and family laid so much store.

His military career reached what was in the circumstances a grotesque anticlimax when he was promoted to the rank of corporal in November 1876. It is the singular conclusion of a singular and unorthodox story. That he did not receive this promotion for zeal in his military duties is evident; and it must be assumed that the award was made on account of his secretarial work.

What is most notable and significant at this stage of his life's history is that a period which produced so much discontent and exasperation should, precisely on that account, have resulted in a reaction which was to have the most salutary effect upon his future career. The bondage and servitude of the army which he so much detested were, in the result, the beginning of a new life. His studies at Clermont-Ferrand to which he was driven by boredom and frustration were the primary foundation of his life's work. Alphonse Bertillon was not one of those whose work was inspired by optimistic enthusiasm. It was an exasperated pessimism which continually drove him on. An acute inferiority complex in the proper sense of that abused term was also a painful spur to endeavour. He felt inferior, not because he was so in fact, but on account of his defective power of social adaptation, which left him isolated and thus haunted by the kind of fears which attack those who are obliged, unaided, to work out their own salvation. If superficially he had acquired a few social graces and if foreign travel had a little softened the harsher outlines of his social attitude, he yet remained fundamentally that "bad character" which even his greatest friends could not fail to recognize. It was his inspiration. Without it he might have lived and died a minor official in some obscure department of the Paris Prefecture.

9. THE SECRET SHRINE

There is a lady sweet and kind.
Was never face so pleased my mind.
I did but see her passing by,
And yet I love her till I die . . . .

Her free behaviour, winning looks
Would make a lawyer burn his books.
I touched her not, alas, not I. . . .

Anon.

IN order to report a certain matter of great significance in his life we have to go forward in time to the death of Alphonse Bertillon. The reason for this is that an event which followed his death has probably deprived the world of evidence concerning the only romantic affair which ever influenced his affective life. By nature a reserved and even a secretive man, the circumstances all conspired to make the secret die with him. It is likely enough that he would have wished it so. On the other hand, it is highly probable that his private papers contained some information which would not have embarrassed him, and which, indeed, he might have been glad to think would have been made known after his death.

This doubtful and ambiguous state of things throws a responsibility upon those who honour his memory. But it is one which cannot be evaded, because, among so much which is problematical, it is certain that this romantic affair was the turning point in his life. It gave shape to what had been a vague and purely theoretical goal. In short, the problem child of the family, at this stage, determined to make a career for himself. No doubt there were subsidiary drives, but at the bottom of it was a woman who was *fons et origo*.

This veil of secrecy might have been lifted at least a little had it not been for something which occurred perhaps very soon after his death at No. 5 Avenue President Wilson, where he had lived. There was a woman in the Bertillon dining-room, a small, neat-looking person, with small, neat features. She might once have been pretty in a prim, unspectacular fashion. Now the hair was almost white, but, from the fast-vanishing tints in it, it seemed that once it was blonde. She wore glasses with very powerful lenses.

The woman stood near an ugly iron stove common to most French houses at that time, its iron piping being the beginning of a chimney which wound through the house to warm it. It was February and cold.

She had at her side bundles of papers neatly tied and docketed. The woman did not open the bundles to look at them. She seemed almost in fear of touching them, and she was muttering to herself. Presently, summoning her courage, she opened the lid of the stove and thrust the packets almost fiercely into the fire.

" There, they are gone. Perhaps now the enemies will leave me alone, leave me alone." She began to weep.

Around her stood the carefully house-kept and rather dreadful ' imperial ' furniture—the great man's æsthetic sense had never been highly developed. But there were contrasts. Upon the wall was the graceful clock which had been a present to him from the Czar of all the Russias. She had also once feared this, wondering when it first came if it had a bomb concealed in it. The clock ticked remorselessly on.

There were a good many papers tightly packed, so that they must have made a considerable smoke. No passer-by in the Avenue President Wilson, seeing the thick emanation from the chimney, could have guessed that good pages of history were vanishing upward to meet the low-lying sullen clouds of that February day.

To the biographer poor crazy Amélie, wife of Alphonse Bertillon, may have much to answer for. It seems strange and tragic that a woman whose mind which, however limited its scope, was so well organized, should have lost her reason solely on account of losing him; but at his death her small but well-ordered universe immediately collapsed in ruins. Utterly devoted to him, she had built no life of her own apart from his, and when he was buried the world of reality went to the grave with him. The substitute which the troubled mind constructed was peopled with ill-wishers and enemies, who, having deprived her of Alphonse, were now conspiring together to injure her. His private possessions which he had not shared with her were a danger.

For there is no reason to believe that she destroyed revengefully correspondence which probably included a number of letters written to him by another woman. It is improbable that she went through that correspondence before burning it, or that, in the state she then was, she would have understood it if she had. But, however that may be, and whatever that packet contained, Amélie Bertillon deprived posterity at one stroke of valuable evidence concerning the life of her husband. With so poor a correspondent and so reserved a man, we cannot afford to be without anything privately written to him. This is to put the matter at its lowest. What has been lost probably included writings relating to the major drama of his emotional life.

In fact, it is much worse than that. With him, as with all such men, affective drives, however jealously concealed, are so closely linked to the total achievement that ignorance of them means serious loss in appreciation of both man and work. Most things are uncertain concerning the affair of Bertillon with his Swedish lady; but it is not uncertain that her influence upon him, at an impressionable period of early manhood, was decisive. The circumstances and events conspire to expose that as a fact.

It is at least certain that he met her in Paris in 1879, for there is no evidence that he was away from the city at that time. Her name is not known, nor any of her connexions, but he admitted to having a photograph which probably went to ashes with the rest in the ugly stove. He had shown it to close friends without disclosing the name.

It is possible to hazard a guess as to the quality of this girl, and as to what her style and sensibility (as he might then have called it) must have been. Within certain limits, the circumstances would have determined that. Although not academically qualified, Bertillon was made a member of the Society of Anthropology in 1878. This already renowned institution had a School of Anthropology attached to it. At that School, by this time internationally recognized—besides his father— Guillard, Broca, Havilaeque, and Topinard, with many other distinguished votaries of the vital sciences, used to lecture there. Other lecturers came from abroad.

Although Alphonse Bertillon had had little systematized scientific training, and at that time no scientific work or success of any kind, as the son of his father he mixed freely with the learned circle and held his own in it. The stay in England, the first medical at the university, and even the military service had refined his barbarism, and given birth to a self-assurance which he never developed to excess, but which gave him a certain poise. In some respects he had matured rapidly for his years, and he had that quality of instinctive judgment which made it possible for him to meet his seniors on their own ground without any appearance of presumption on his part.

He was tall and well-built with features in a classical mould, and in general he had the face and outline which any woman might have looked at twice. Nothing is more probable than that the blonde creature of his dreams was the daughter of some Swedish savant who had come to see and hear what was being done at the new school which Dr Bertillon and his colleagues had made notable as an intellectual centre.

It was known to the Bertillons generally that the girl belonged to a distinguished family, and this meant, by any Bertillon definition, one which was distinguished intellectually, for no other kind of distinction was recognized by them. Taking it altogether, it is a reasonable guess that she was a professor's daughter.

Or perhaps a wife. It is no reflection upon his memory to suggest this. He was even a little obtrusively ascetic all his life through. The very essence of the romance and its inspiration was the impossibility of fulfilment in any concrete and physical sense. This was fully in tune with his romantic style at that time, and for that matter with a good deal of the romanticism of his period.

Dr Bertillon, who had his share of shrewdness and common sense, knew something of the matter, and doubtless inferred a great deal more. Concerned more with effects than causes, he made no attempt to overcome his son's wary reserve.

The side-effects were that Alphonse no longer drifted so aimlessly along, absorbed with dreams which were not even intended to come true. He began systematically to attend courses of lectures at the School, and showed particular interest in ethnography. The doctor received a hint from Reclus, the geographer, that something serious was afoot. Alphonse had asked him for help with references. He was taking life and study more seriously. Reclus did not disclose what had been told him in confidence—that Alphonse contemplated writing a book, which was afterwards to be published as *Les Races Sauvages*.

More concerned with these encouraging results than with the inspiration behind them, Dr Bertillon was satisfied. His grand-daughter, Suzanne Bertillon, probing deeper, gives an explanation of this more constructive enthusiasm, and new will to work :

Il n'était pas comme les autres. . . . Il lui semblait que la jolie Suédoise appartînt à une autre sphère, à une sphère sublime dont la lumière irradiait autour d'elle si violemment qu'elle faisait oublier tout chagrin, toute déception, et communiquait a l'âme et à l'esprit un élan nouveau: le désir d'une action d'éclat, le désir d'une victoire. Son ambition avait des ailes, et voulait réaliser quelque chose de grand et le lui offrir un hommage de dévotion.

If this is an accurate diagnosis—and there could be none more authoritative—this was no empty romanticism and calf-love, but the utilization of an emotional drive to impose a form and pattern upon life and work. On this evidence, it would be characteristic of Bertillon that had there been no Swedish girl—real, but in a last resort inaccessible—he would have been obliged to create one, because some such symbol was necessary to achieve success and fame.

It is not known how often they met, or how many letters passed between them, but it is known that the correspondence went on for some time. Likely enough hers played up to a situation she understood, and urged a promising young hero on. She may well have been the hidden force behind *Les Races Sauvages*. This is not a very good book, but it marks an important stage in the progress of a man who was to achieve so much.

Unhappily, this is all that we know of one of the most significant chapters in the life of Alphonse Bertillon. It is vital, because, whatever else is doubtful, there is certainty that it had a powerful and decisive influence upon his future.

There is one other interesting fact which it is not possible to interpret with confidence. In July 1893 he was awarded the Swedish Order of Wasa. This was the first foreign distinction he ever received, and it preceded the award of the Blue Ribbon of the Legion, which was not conferred upon him by France until October of the same year. Some special recommendation must have been behind this gesture. Although Bertillon was to find recognition in every European country, he received no other from abroad for three years, the next being the Order of Orange-Nassau of Holland in 1896.

It has been suggested, and it is, of course, not impossible, that the hand of his young Swedish friend was in this. But, if so, it is difficult to explain how it comes about that his closely guarded secret has remained unrevealed until this day. Further speculation would lead nowhere. Historically the most interesting fact is that the country to which his romantic imagination must have been most closely linked should have been the first to recognize and reward his scientific work.

PART THREE

THE WORK

10. THE PREFECTURE CLERK

BERTILLON might have become a great physician or anthropologist if the course of his general education had run more smoothly. For this rough passage he had largely himself to blame. In the result, the passing of his *baccalauréat* at the late age of twenty made it difficult for him to pursue an academic course. Normally he could have followed his medical studies for at least two years, uninterrupted by military service. But, owing to this delay in matriculation, his military duty clashed with his needs as a university student at an important stage. This may explain his failure to follow up the success of his ' first medical.' A young man in good health would have had the necessary physical stamina to study systematically and serve in the army at the same time. Alphonse Bertillon was not in good health. He suffered frequently from acute migraine and serious nose-bleeding. At the conclusion of his military service, when he may still have been considering, late as it was, a return to the university, he was struck down with typhoid fever. It was a dangerous illness with a long and difficult convalescence.

With these set-backs, he was to learn the hard way. Bertillon was a rebel, but even in his most difficult phase he was not a time-wasting dilettante. Recovered from his illness, he saw his brothers and friends each pursuing a career and doing systematic work of some kind, while he was without training, without work, and with no clear vision of a career—with, in fact, nothing more solid than a vague if vast aspiration to be "a man of Science." It was a mortifying experience, but a salutary one. The realistically hard head he had inherited from his mother began to assert itself. He became, before all else, determined to earn a livelihood.

Dr Bertillon was concerned about the future of his wayward, difficult son. An intellectual himself, he knew that Alphonse had a brain if a way to canalize its activity could only be found. Whatever he did for a living, he must be encouraged to cultivate his scientific habit of mind. His success in the first medical proved that he had capacity, even in the scholastic sense. He proposed his son as a member of the Anthropological Society, of which he was a vice-president. This was rewarded with enthusiasm and gratitude when he was elected. What Dr Bertillon did not know was that the young man was still intensively reading the anatomy of which he had made so encouraging a success at Clermont-Ferrand.

Alphonse hid his closest intellectual interests under a bushel, and tended to withhold them even from his father. In spite of his grandiloquent visions, he was fundamentally modest and uncertain of himself. It held him back from discussing freely the intellectual enthusiasms which were nearest to his heart. His device for covering them at that time was his sincere anxiety, which he knew his father shared, to make a career for himself. . . .

" I am nearly twenty-six, and not trained for anything; but I want a job, Papa, so that I can earn my living. Can't you find me something, however small, to start with? "

Dr Bertillon was pleased, and a little taken aback. Never before had his son asked him such a thing. With a graceless obedience he had gone to the bank as a clerk, only to leave it after three months under a thunder-cloud. His father knew that he would have done the same thing again if pushed to it, and with the same result, or worse. This initiative was a new and more promising portent.

" *Incipit vita nova*," murmured the doctor. " We will see what can be done."

Alphonse, who had hated the classics, at least understood this. It would be a new life, and he was probably not going to enjoy it, but at the same time something like a small hope began to dawn.

Because of his medical and statistical work for the Municipality, Dr Bertillon had some influence in the matter of minor official appointments. At that time a vacancy occurred in one of the departments of the Prefecture of Police. On March 15, 1879, Alphonse Bertillon became a clerk in the *premier bureau*. His duties were to copy out forms.

The hard and stony road had begun. With his disordered background, the young man had a particular horror of routine and repetitive clerical work. But the idle years with their spacious indiscipline were over, and he had to pay for them. . . .

The price, as he was soon to find, was high. General conditions and organization in the office of the Prefect of Police left a good deal to be desired. In order to understand the revolution which this junior employee brought about, almost single-handed, in four years, the background must be sketched in.

The methods of the French police in that year of grace 1879 had changed very little in principle from those initiated by that criminal turned policeman, the brilliant and unscrupulous Vidocq. They consisted in the liberal use of the police informer and *agent provocateur*. At the beginning of the nineteenth and indeed until the middle of the century, the police had no real interest in systematic methods for the detection of crime, since they were fully occupied with the detection and arrest of political suspects. There was therefore little incentive to improve the general methods of detection or the recording of movements and activities of law-breakers which are the foundation of modern criminal investigation.

The problem of identification was almost entirely neglected. Up to 1832 in France a barbarous method of identification of criminals was still permitted by the statute; they could be branded with a red-hot iron. For minor offences, which might never have been repeated, a man was thus marked as a criminal for life, and in consequence he remained one of necessity. In practice this wicked process had been abandoned some time before. There is a traditional anecdote, concerning the ingenious Vidocq, which suggests that it was not in current use in his day. His custom when he went to clean up a den of thieves was to stand at the door as they passed out of the raided premises. He then deftly marked those whom he recognized as habitually bad characters on the back of their clothing with white chalk. On seeing this mark, his officers then arrested them at the exit of the building.

Branding had thus at least ceased to be universal in 1809. No systematized method of identification, barbarous or otherwise, replaced it.

None worthy of the name had been evolved by 1879. It was impossible to take seriously such descriptions as ' average ' and ' ordinary' in describing height or limb. About 1840 photographs were added to the physiological description (if it can properly be called that), which as often as not disproved the fallacy that the camera never lies. The method used in actual practice to identify an individual who had been in the hands of the police before was not very creditable to the inventors. When individuals or groups arrived to serve their sentence an officer was posted to greet them on their entrance as if they were old friends in the hope that this unexpected geniality might betray the prisoner into some admission that he had been in prison before.

We can presume that this dishonest and clumsy method must occasionally have been successful. It must invariably have failed with all but the most simple-minded had it not been for an artistic piece of corruption which was added to it. A payment of five francs was offered to every officer for each offender whom he recognized as having previously been in the hands of the law. The result of this was a widespread practice of compounding felonies. Corrupt officers induced prisoners to admit to a previous conviction on the promise of a share of the five-franc piece.

But the forms remained to crown this corrupt and rickety structure. No one took them seriously, but the ritual of filling them in continued. This was the duty of the unfortunate young Bertillon. He carried it out from 8 o'clock in the morning until 6 o'clock at night for a salary of about £50 a year. He hated those forms, and there was little consolation in the knowledge that his hatred was righteous. They were an insult to everything that he had learnt, heard, or seen concerning scientific method. Also they outraged the social conscience he had inherited and acquired from his father and grandfather and perhaps from many generations of Bertillons and

Guillards. But the Bertillon spirit moved him to turn that hatred to a constructive end. He was determined to produce a form which really meant something.

That resolution taken, his work became a matter of facetious or puzzled speculation among a staff who were not conspicuous for imagination. They had never understood their retiring and remote colleague, whose manner was generally brusque, often to the point of rudeness. When he began to cut up photographs and juxtapose the isolated features of different individuals by mounting them side by side on pieces of cardboard some of them even began to touch their heads significantly. Such is the resistance of those tightly bound by a meaningless routine to anything new that perhaps it is not surprising that many of them sincerely thought him mad. This idea was strengthened when it became known that he was writing a report to be submitted to the Prefect. The fellow had been in the department only eight months! None the less, that report went in on October 1, 1879.

He had made a discovery. Quite simply stated, it was that it could be proved by means of a series of measurements of the body that no two human individuals were exactly alike. Using the statistical techniques which Quételet, his father, and grandfather had taught him, he had applied them not for the purpose of classifying humanity in groups, but for that of isolating the individuals each from the other and showing them to be in some respects unique. These measurements, reduced to formulæ, could be recorded upon a form which was really significant, because it was the essential portrait of the person described and of none other.

The proof of this was sustained by elementary mathematical concepts which, while they were perfectly clear to Bertillon, meant very little to the Prefect of Police. M. Andrieux was a man of very moderate scholastic attainments who had secured his post by family and political influence. Mathematics had never been his strong point. Presumably such words as 'binomial' and 'geometrical progression' were remembered from a distant past, and he may possibly have vaguely recognized the distribution curves, but that they could possibly have any significance for his department was incredible. A man, innocent of mathematics, who sees a cone-shaped object carefully drawn upon a piece of paper by a young clerk with a reputation for eccentricity may perhaps be excused the conclusion that he is the victim of an elaborate practical joke, or that his correspondent is out of his mind.

The Prefect believed the latter. He ignored the first report, but when the troublesome young clerk returned to the attack with a second, more detailed and perhaps more incomprehensible than the first, M. Andrieux decided to act. He sent for Bertillon. It was not at all the sort of interview which the young enthusiast had pictured.

" Bertillon? I believe you are a clerk of the twentieth grade, and on the staff eight months, eh? And you have ideas, it seems. Your report reads like a practical joke."

" If you will allow me to explain, sir——"

" Well? "

This was precisely what Alphonse Bertillon could not do. He was one of those men who never could learn to make an exposition properly adjusted to the level of a non-technical and especially an unsympathetic audience. He had an unsympathetic audience now, and he was horribly nervous. The explanation was not a success.

" So you think our system of records can be improved by your method. Of course, I don't understand what your method is; but I doubt it. We have used the method we have for a long time, and have considerable experience. It works very well."

Disappointed and mortified as he was, Alphonse Bertillon spoke his mind. It was his dangerous habit.

" If you will excuse me, sir, it doesn't work well; it doesn't work at all. I know. I have to fill in the forms."

M. Andrieux was an unimaginative bureaucrat, but he was not a fool. This tactless remark exasperated him the more because he knew it was true.

" M. Bertillon," he said, " you are a young man in a junior position in this department, and with no experience of it. You have no scientific qualifications, and you produce an incomprehensible report which you cannot explain. I warn you that if I am troubled again I shall take a serious view of it."

The unlucky interview was at an end. But the results of it were worse than this first bitter blow to the young man's hopes. The letter which the Prefect of Police wrote to Dr Bertillon has not been preserved, but its contents are known. It expressed the opinion that the state of Alphonse Bertillon's mind should be inquired into, and that in any case if he persisted in writing absurd reports of the type with which they had been troubled his appointment would be terminated.

Dr Bertillon was seriously disturbed. After the disastrous school reports, and the very unpleasant letter he had received from the secretary of the bank, his son's last employer in France, this seemed to be the herald of another catastrophe. In the evening of the day after the interview he produced the letter.

"You had better read this, and tell me what it means."

If the interview had been a shock to Alphonse the letter was a worse one. For some time he could only look at his father without speaking. Then he brought it out.

"So he thinks I am mad. It's the reports. Perhaps I have made a mess of it. I ought to have shown the reports to you, and asked your advice before I sent them in. I have copies—will you read them? I don't know why I didn't come to you —but I have to work these things out for myself."

"Yes. I will read them." Dr Bertillon felt suddenly relieved. This, at least, was not a repetition of previous disasters. Perhaps there was more in this than met the eye.

Without a word Alphonse took some papers from his pocket, and handed them to his father. The trained eye of the anthropologist quickly scanned the reports page by page. Then he looked at his son almost as if he were seeing him for the first time.

"I want to read these at once," he said. "Come back in an hour."

When Alphonse returned the atmosphere had changed. His father was a just man, and he had been angry. He was not angry now.

"I must apologize, Alphonse. When I read the Prefect's letter I thought you had been up to your—ah—practical jokes again. I have read your reports. They are not a joke. I think

you have made a very interesting discovery. Of course, I
knew you were interested in anthropology and statistics, but I
never dreamt that you were going practically to apply what
you have learnt from us in a new field."

Father and son were among those sensitive and reserved
people who do not wear their hearts on their sleeves. But
Alphonse could see that his father was very strongly moved.
He felt acutely embarrassed.

" I—well—I only wanted to straighten out some things in
the department." Even as he spoke he knew that this was not
the whole truth. The large and confused visions of his adolescence were beginning to take form and shape. His father took
words out of his mouth which he could not have formulated.

" There is much more in it than that. You are going to
identify lawbreakers with your measurements. Good! But we
are also going to be able to prove that every man and woman
born into this world is an unique specimen. We can para-
phrase Napoleon's words: ' *La statisque, c'est le budget des
hommes et des femmes, et sans ce budget, point de salut
public.*' "

Dr Bertillon seldom allowed himself such a demonstration,
but he got up, embraced his son, and kissed him. There were
tears in his eyes.

ANDRIEUX, Prefect of Police, had said no, and what had begun as a matter of conviction was soon to become a question of official dignity. Convictions can be altered; *amour propre* is more difficult to combat. Dr Bertillon had not been idle. He was the President of the Society of Anthropology with the important school attached to it which he had also founded, and he began to spread the news of his son's inventions in circles which it was not easy to ignore. M. Andrieux became uncomfortably aware through a number of reliable sources that there was, after all, some method in the madness of his troublesome clerk. From contemptuous dismissal of the matter he was now in the position of trying to protect himself against it.

To be fair to the Prefect, he was not animated by mere prejudice. An official who had become entangled in the mechanisms he devised and maintained, he was not alone in resisting these new and revolutionary theories. Gustave Macé, hero of the notorious Voirbo case, was chief of the Detective Division. A man of great intelligence and even brilliance, he was wedded to the classical methods of his period, and looked with great suspicion upon scientific methods, which he thought too theoretical to be of any value in the day-by-day practice of detection. He disliked the remote Byronic young man, who could not leave well alone, and disliked still more the dangerous innovations he was trying to force upon an unwilling Prefecture. Every policeman on the beat to-day knows that scientific methods form a necessary part of the practical work of criminal investigation. It was a very different matter in 1879, and not in France only. Although no one at the Prefecture knew of it, and Bertillon was ignorant of the matter himself, a member of the Indian Civil Service had discovered

fourteen years before that the patterns on the finger-ends
served to identify the individual. Herschel was treated in
exactly the same way as Bertillon, except that no one accused
him of being insane. The higher authorities to whom Herschel
submitted his report were not sufficiently impressed even to be
irritated. They ignored the matter altogether, and nothing
more was heard of it for ten years.

But, while Herschel shrugged off his disappointment,
Alphonse Bertillon sat sullenly at his desk and became a more
difficult colleague than ever. He was wanting in that divine
gift of patience which imaginative men so often lack and
which yet they badly need. As it often is with boys who are
troublesome at school, Alphonse had set himself to be a conscientious worker. His superiors never had cause to complain
on that score. But the forms he completed, once disliked, were
now loathed. Not only did he know them to be futile, but he
now had a constructive remedy vouched for by his father,
whose judgment in such matters was final.

He was extremely unpopular with his colleagues, who
disliked and feared an aloofness which was occasionally
punctuated with barbed sarcasm. They could not be expected
to understand that his prickly nature stemmed from a fundamental shyness and frustration in social adjustment. It was
attributed to the ambition of the official climber who was
utilizing external pressure to rise over their heads. They could
hardly be expected to judge him by standards not their own,
and so realize that his ambition was innocent of ordinary
worldly motive; that he was obsessed by the ' discovery ' and
wanted only an opportunity to find out how it would work.
Even less than the Prefect could they understand what the
discovery was.

He was thus condemned to what seemed to him the monstrous farce of writing out what purported to be descriptions
of human beings. These, in fact, described nothing human
nor indeed anything at all in the heavens above or in the
earth beneath or in the waters under the earth. We begin to
sympathize with the young man's exasperation the more as we
realize that he did not think of the ' discovery' as a mere
device to keep track of the lawbreaker. Bertillon was before

all else an individualist in the more refined sense of the word. His discovery was a reflexion of his passionate conviction that everything which lived and moved under heaven was in some respects unique. He had absorbed this inspiration from his father and grandfather, who in turn had it as a heritage from the scientific humanism of their time.

Meanwhile Louis-Alphonse Bertillon, more saint-like and yet more worldly-wise than his son ever became, counselled patience. "As long as Andrieux is Prefect," he said, "we shall never be able to introduce anthropological methods into your department. But Andrieux won't last for ever. I don't think his successor, even if he wanted to, will be able to ignore this. Even the delay may be a good thing. Work it all out in detail so that you are ready for the test when it comes."

Alphonse took this advice. Impatient of delay, he was not impatient where the *magnum opus* was concerned. The most notable characteristic of the Bertillon system is its theoretical simplicity. Bertillon's genius was not in the realm of abstract thinking. But this defect (so to call it) only served to consoli-date the system he devised. *Bertillonage* is elaborate without being complicated, scientific in principle and yet intelligible to any man of intellectual integrity and common sense. He created and shaped it so. Profiting by his experience with his sceptical chief, he concentrated upon the practical aspects of the problem. If there are, say, one thousand men in a small town whose height is 1.65 metres how many of these will also have a head 187 millimetres long and 153 millimetres wide? How many measurements must be made to find a formula which will fit one individual only?

He bought instruments, calipers such as his father used for the larger measurements, and pincer gauges for the smaller. No one knows how and when he made his first experiments. The unsympathetic attitude of his chief does not suggest that he could have found complacent guinea-pigs among his colleagues in the department, but what is certain is that he had already decided that to pinpoint the individual specimen he would require eleven measurements. He had chosen those parts of the body which could most easily be measured accurately. They were the length and breadth of the head,

F

and of the right ear, the length from the elbow to the end of
the middle finger, that of the middle and ring fingers themselves; the length of the left foot, the height, the length of the
trunk (*buste*), and that of the outstretched arms from middle
to middle finger-end.

Most probably his victims in the cause of science were his
father's friends and his fellow members of the Society of
Anthropology. By way of example he did not hesitate to be
hoist with his own petard. There is more than one photograph
of him including the complete anthropometric description and
the *portrait parlé*.

The *portrait parlé* was, accidentally, his greatest achievement. Bertillon originally made it part of his system because
he was not satisfied that there was any practical means of
identifying an individual by measurement alone. The reason
for this scepticism was probably his insecure grasp of the
mathematics of the process. There is evidence that he never
fully understood the principles of the calculus of probability.
His father had accumulated a vast quantity of statistical
material. On the basis of this Bertillon could have deduced
that the probability of two individuals of the same height
being identical was of the order of 4 to 1, and that with every
additional measurement which corresponded, the probability
of identity would increase, as mathematicians say, as 4^n—
that is to say, by the progressive multiplication of the original
odds by 4. By this calculation he would have found that the
chances against two different individuals having eleven
measurements in common would be 4,194,304 to 1. Bertillon
must, of course, have understood this in principle, but if he
had been fully satisfied of its validity in practice, he would
have seen that the simplest method of making his system
practically infallible would have been to increase the number
of measurements to, say, 14. The chances against a mistake
in identity would then have risen to 268,435,456 to 1. These
odds are so high as to make identity a practical certainty.

But for this doubt we might have been deprived of that
part of his work which has outlived his first discovery. It
explains the cutting up of the photograph which his colleagues
first thought was one of his little eccentricities and which later

they called derisively the *portrait parlé*. Many a true word is spoken in jest, for a ' speaking likeness ' was precisely what Alphonse Bertillon was aiming at. The kind of photograph which accompanied the old cards was practically useless. Photography, as Bertillon devised it, was standardized and accurate. He planned to photograph every accused person in full face and profile, which was in itself an important innovation. On the bases of these photographs the design of face and features was accurately described, the existence of special marks such as scars or warts was noted. Added to the description was the colour of the eyes and of the hair and the manner of its growth.

In one sense, the young man was preparing a rod for his own back. The scheme called for a large amount of systematic detail work. Bertillon hated this and continued to hate the mechanical aspect of his system. But behind all that lay the consolation that, however irksome the routine processes might be, the experiments were establishing something vital, not only concerning men who were accused of crime but about mankind in particular and in general. At the root of Bertillon's success there was a human as well as a scientific impulse. His professional activity was restricted to the criminal field; but, in fact, the real focus of his interest was mankind and the human individual. In a last resort, the crimes committed were no concern of his. A man of his type inevitably found a kind of romance in a technique the aim of which was to individualize human beings. This may well account for the personal status and respect which he won from his countrymen without seeking it, or even knowing that he had done so.

In March 1892 an incident occurred which reveals this quality in the man lying beneath the cold and ferocious exterior. It has been recorded of him that he was always courteous to those whom he had to photograph. On the 27th of that month the dandified ruffian Koeningstein, better known as Ravachol, was arrested and brought in. He was a criminal anarchist, accused of two murders and two bomb-outrages which had seriously wounded a number of people. The prisoner looked far from dandified on this occasion. His face was bruised and bleeding, and his clothing in disorder.

Ravachol had furiously resisted arrest, and declared that if he were to be photographed it would be by force.

"Why?" said Bertillon. "I have to do this. It is part of my duty."

Ravachol had fought with the police, and had been very roughly handled. He was taken aback at the quiet question and the calm statement.

"I won't be photographed now."

"And why not now?"

"My face is not a very pretty sight, is it?" This was the root of the matter. He wanted to look his best even in a police photograph.

Bertillon smiled. "You are right. We will put it off. After all, what I want is a true likeness."

This might have been nothing more than a professional gesture; but it was not this which caused the Chief of the Department of Judicial Identity to send his client a mounted copy of the photograph after he had taken it some days later.

It touched the man who had defied examining magistrates and judges and who went to the scaffold shouting "Long live the Revolution!"

"M. Bertillon," he said, "at least, is a gentleman."

It was entirely characteristic of him to treat the law-breaker with consideration, and to reserve his irony and sarcasm for his colleagues and peers. Even in those earlier days the Bertillon manner had become proverbial. It probably delayed the promotion grudgingly given to him on January 8, 1881. His conscientiousness and efficiency could not be denied. Perhaps, also, his superiors were a little afraid of him.

Bertillon's foot was on the second rung of the ladder.

12. THE UNOFFICIAL SECRETARY

THE winter of 1881 distracted Alphonse Bertillon with hopes and fears. His promotion meant very little to him. It had been accompanied by threatening hints that if he persisted in trying to disorganize the department with his ideas and theories he might be down-graded.

His book, *Les Races Sauvages*, was a way of escape. He completed it at that time. Published in 1882, it cannot be said that it did much to enhance his reputation. Literature was not his *métier*, and the subject was one of which he had a very elementary grasp. Written as a popular work, it was more popular with its author than his public. Alphonse Bertillon was quite aware of its defects, and it is perhaps surprising that he should have published a work which he never took very seriously. His own comment throws light upon the matter: "It interested and amused me at a difficult time."

He was walking one of those winter days—it was to prove an occasion—down the Rue de Rivoli, where he had been born twenty-eight years before. Meticulously neat but rather sombre clothing had become a habit with him; but he had developed what he never lost, a kind of elegance and distinction in the oddest contrast with his abrupt and unpolished manners.

Alphonse Bertillon shared with his father that kind of intense preoccupation which could at times make him oblivious of his surroundings. He saw now not the street, but perhaps long lines of noses, ears, and mouths, which grouped themselves in a common order and yet were distinct each one. Why should anyone think it strange or eccentric to look at the human face in this fashion, and tell him that he was a theorist and a crank?

Rue des Pyramides . . . when he paused at the crossing

Alphonse suddenly became aware of some one close to him, and a voice.

" Will you have the great kindness to help me cross the street? I am very short-sighted and afraid of the traffic."

The young man started violently. He was afraid of real women, and the more embarrassed that one had spoken to him in the public highway. Then he looked and saw a blonde girl, short and slim, with a fresh complexion. She seemed dreadfully embarrassed herself, but she smiled at him. He noted with professional interest the small, even teeth.

" Take my arm." This was done as he suddenly remembered how his mother had rallied him because he was too shy to take hers in the Tuileries.

They were safely, and to her almost miraculously, over. She thanked him, making as if to hurry away. Something about her touched him. It might, of course, have been the mild weather with sunshine promising spring, or it might have been that he intuitively perceived the significance of this small event. He spoke more gruffly than usual.

" Comment vous appellez vous, mademoiselle? "

" Moi, je m'appelle Amélie—Amélie Notar. Et vous? "

" Alphonse—Alphonse Bertillon."

He had caught her foreign accent. The adventures of her recent history came out. She was Austrian and had not been long in Paris. With but one introduction from her parish priest, she had no friends, and she earned her living by giving German lessons. Even in those days not all women were sheltered.

The young man had forgotten his shyness, and so became charming, as he could, when the defences were down. The candour and directness which endeared him to his friends came through.

" I want to learn German. I have tried and tried. Perhaps you could take me as a pupil."

It was arranged there and then. If Dr Bertillon ever had any doubts as to whether it was really German that this little Austrian girl who had (so to say) picked his son up in the street wanted to teach they must have been dispelled when he met her. She was simple and unassuming, and yet she had a great force of character. If it is true of any woman that she achieves her influence by stooping to conquer it was true of her. In any case, as it turned out, there was no doubt about the German. Alphonse, who had hated the subject at school, as he had hated most others, was talking German in a few months.

Amélie Notar achieved much more than this. She never tried to break through his reserve, nor was she disturbed by the long and obstinate silences wherewith their conversation was punctuated. Thus she overcame his fear of committing himself, and he began to talk of his discovery and his hopes concerning it and of his problems at the Prefecture.

Few women at this time knew anything of science; but, perhaps precisely because anthropology was a high mystery, his prestige, considerable already, was vastly enhanced. But if she thought of Alphonse Bertillon as one of those above the common sort and an initiate of higher mysteries she was quick to see the method and order inherent in his discovery. Her own mind worked in the same way. She liked to classify and label everything.

At first he would not take her offer of collaboration seriously. He was won over because of her small, neat, and rapid handwriting. One of the most bitter of the complaints of his schoolmasters and one of the justest was the Bertillon calligraphy. As a Prefecture clerk he had managed to improve it, as the cards he himself wrote show; but handwriting remained a horrifying process. Amélie Notar became his secretary.

He dictated to her *Les Races Sauvages* from his indecipherable manuscript. At a period when shorthand was little used she had evolved a system of her own. The fair copy which was to go to the printers was clear and legible from the first word to the last.

She took it as a matter of course that this genius was very soon to come into his own and thereby supplied a self-confidence which was not naturally his. With a pride almost blatantly aping humility, she said that handwriting was her only talent. There would be much to do when the Prefecture adopted the Bertillon method. It was for him to think the things out and for her to write them down.

And, as if in answer to this matter-of-fact prophecy, the thing they were all waiting for presently happened. Monsieur Andrieux, appropriately decorated, retired, and Camecasse, a new Prefect, reigned in his stead.

Dr Bertillon began to pull wires. His son was all for making a frontal attack. Even at twenty-eight, he had not learnt the techniques of diplomacy, and he never did. His father said no. He had interested his friend Edgar Demange, a well-known lawyer, who had great influence at the Prefecture. Ironically enough, Demange was afterwards to take part in the defence of Captain Dreyfus. It might take a little time, but they must be patient. Camecasse was quite different from Andrieux. He had more up-to-date ideas. They waited.

It is characteristic of Bertillon that when summoned to the Prefect's office, as he very soon was, he went there in fear and trembling, wondering if he would be able to explain his method to the satisfaction of his new chief and what would happen if he made a mess of it.

The opening was encouraging. He was smiled upon and asked to sit down. The Prefect had heard of his methods and thought them promising. Could he be told what was the basic principle of this identification technique?

It is doubtful if the oration that followed really made clear to the Prefect the relation between demography, botanical and etymological classifications, and the identification of recidivists. This kind of exposition was not Bertillon's strong point. But he made an impression. Even if the new Prefect was not prepared to take the unknown for granted he was not going to reject out of hand.

" It sounds rather theoretical, Bertillon. Now, I have nothing against that. But we are practical people here, as you must know, having been on the staff for some years."

" I want a chance to try it, sir."

" You are going to have that. From next week we will adopt your methods of identification at the Depot. You can have two clerks, and I will give you three months to identify a recidivist solely by your own method."

If misfortunes never come singly this can also be true of fortunate events. Flying to tell his father the good news, it seemed a good omen that he found him reading the proofs of *Les Races Sauvages*. Jacques and Georges were also there. His older brother had recently published his thesis on the *Demography of Divorce*. The doctor was overjoyed that these strokes of fortune had followed so closely upon each other. It made him feel, he said, ten years younger. Louis-Adolphe Bertillon was in need of rejuvenation. Suffering from polyarthritis, he had become an invalid, and lay, though he never spoke of it, under the shadow of death; and the year before he had lost his closest colleague and greatest friend, the anthropologist Broca, who was, with him, the most devoted research worker of his day.

They dined *en famille* that night, but festively in their sober fashion, drinking a thought more wine than usual and *le pousse-café*. Auguste Broca, son of the man with large whiskers à la Huxley and the leonine head who had devised anthropological measuring instruments still used to-day, was with them. Auguste was then a student of surgery, as he was afterwards professor of the faculty in the Sorbonne. Since his father's death Dr Bertillon had become, for him, the high priest of the new science. Jacques and Alphonse, his senior contemporaries, were rising stars in the greater firmament.

It was a red-letter day for Alphonse and fortified his none too confident spirit; but if recognition by contemporaries and seniors fortified him for the tasks ahead it was the little Austrian, doing what some might call the donkey work, who was one of the major props which supported him at this vital stage in his career. The two clerks were good enough, but they were little better than conscientious automatons. Amelie worked night and day compiling the records in her clear, neat handwriting. She knew little of anthropology or mathematics, but understood very well what was classification, name and thing. The measurements of the human species at enmity with the law grew apace. Bertillon and his secretary were creating historical records of a type never imagined before.

The studied simplicity of Bertillonage is perhaps its most remarkable characteristic. In practice the problem was to find those parts of the body which could be most quickly and accurately measured with the simplest instruments. The measurements which seem at first sight to be chosen almost at random have a vital characteristic in common—they show definitely and easily recognizable points of reference for measurements with the minimum chances of serious error in working : the height, the length of the finger, the span of the outstretched arms, the length and breadth of the ear, are all measurements which can be made, and if necessary repeated, by operators using instruments in the use of which they could rapidly be made efficient. In this respect Bertillon was the creator of the fundamentals of experimental anthropometric technique. Even to-day the problems of the more elaborate measurements necessary to experimental anthropology have not been completely solved, but it remains true that without the fundamental practice first formulated by Bertillon they would be more formidable than, in fact, they are.

This was but one aspect of the problem of applying the work in practice. The most formidable difficulty to be overcome was the keeping of the records themselves. It is useless to produce intimate portraits of individuals which precisely identify them if the portraits cannot quickly be found when they are required.

To solve this problem Bertillon ingeniously utilized and adapted the anthropological methods of classification which he had learnt from his father. The body and all its parts could be expressed in terms of large, medium, or small. He therefore divided his cards into three groups corresponding first to the length of the head—the first for the large, the second for the medium, and the third for the small heads. These three groups were again subdivided in terms of a large, medium, and small width of the head, making nine groups (3^2) in all. These nine groups were again subdivided in terms of the small, medium, and large left middle-finger, making twenty-seven groups (3^3) in all. The last subdivision was made in terms of the small, medium, and large left little finger. This finally produced eighty-one groups (3^4) in all. A cabinet with eighty-one drawers, with nine horizontal and nine vertical rows, could thus accommodate the anthropometric descriptions of many thousands of individuals with a properly balanced distribution of the cards throughout the drawers. Further, it is obvious that as the combination of measurements increases the area within the cabinet where the combined measurements sought can be found decreases to the point where a single drawer must contain the combination required. The table on p. 92 showing one section of twenty-seven compartments of the cabinet makes the arrangement clear. (See Appendix II.)

These were the essentials of the Bertillon system of classification and system of filing the cards. It is clear that the method reduces the possibility of misfiling a card to the minimum and makes it practicable to find the card required, if it exists, with a very short search.

But the system was developed beyond this point. By an ingenious adaptation of the formal anthropological categories of minimum, average, and maximum size, Bertillon ensured that his filing system should arrange approximately an equal number of cards in each section. He did this by devising arbitrary limits of minimum, average, and maximum size so that the groups could be balanced numerically. It is obvious that in the long run the search of any card-index of this kind will be more easily and quickly made if the sections where the search must be made are substantially of the same size.

The science of identification could never have been applied in practice had it not been possible to devise a system of classification and arrangement which was practically foolproof and which made it possible to find the description required with the minimum loss of time. It is indisputable that Bertillon devised the first system of this type, and that the principles of classification he formulated were utilized in one form or another by all his successors.

It is also indisputable that he carried through this great work because of the help and inspiration he had from the Austrian girl who had taught him German. His niece has summed it up well: " For him the thought; for her the action."

This action produced a steady growth of the beautifully written cards during the probationary period, and with them grew the hopes and fears of the partners in this new experiment. With Alphonse it was mainly a fear which grew. By this time he knew enough of the practical application of the

Length of the Head	Width of the Head	Length of Middle Finger	Length of Little Finger	Drawer No.
α – 18.3	α – 15.2	α – 10.9	α – 8.0	1
			8.1 – 8.3	2
			8.4 – ω	3
		11.0 – 11.4	α – 8.5	4
			8.6 – 8.8	5
			8.9 – ω	6
		11.5 – ω	α – 8.9	7
			9.0 – 9.2	8
			9.3 – ω	9
	15.3 – 15.7	α – 11.0	α – 8.2	10
			8.3 – 8.5	11
			8.6 – ω	12
		11.1 – 11.4	α – 8.5	13
			8.6 – 8.8	14
			8.9 – ω	15
		11.5 – ω	α – 9.0	16
			9.1 – 9.3	17
			9.4 – ω	18
	15.8 – ω	α – 11.1	α – 8.2	19
			8.3 – 8.5	20
			8.6 – ω	21
		11.2 – 11.6	α – 8.7	22
			8.8 – 8.9	23
			9.0 – ω	24
		11.7 – ω	α – 9.1	25
			9.2 – 9.4	26
			9.5 – ω	27

α = lower limit   ω = upper limit

principles of probability to realize that, putting it at its highest, the statistical chances of a previous convict returning to the fold within three months were about equal. If the chances went against him they would say that the method was not reliable, that some individual who had been 'inside' before must have been missed. They might refuse to extend the period of grace and abandon the experiment altogether. Two months had already gone by. Nothing.

It was a gloomy day in February 1883. He was at his blackest, his mood conforming well with the gloom of the morning outside. Even the clients had a depressing appearance of uniformity. He had measured six Duponts. At that moment he was engaged with the sixth. It was late in the afternoon, near the time when he officially ceased work.

He looked at the sixth Dupont, and it struck him that he had seen that face before. The method whereby he studied them convinced him that he could never forget a face. In this example, besides the features, there was a mole near the left eyebrow. But where? It might have been in the street or in a bus.

Length of the head 187 millimetres, width 156 millimetres; middle finger 114 millimetres; little finger 89 millimetres . . . it is said that when he went to the cabinet to check these measurements he was trembling violently. Excellent though his memory was, he could hardly have recalled these figures among so many; but he was convinced that the moment had arrived.

It was a medium head, so that only the middle section of the cabinet need be searched. The breadth measurement narrowed the number of drawers to nine, the length of the middle finger to three, of the little finger to one. There were fifty cards in it, and he found it there. The name was Martin, convicted on December 15, 1882. Bertillon was not yet satisfied that the photographs he was taking were sufficiently exact, but he was satisfied with this one. It clearly showed the mole near the left eyebrow. He looked rapidly over the remaining details upon the card and suddenly shouted with laughter when he noted the nature of the previous conviction. It appealed to his sense of the grotesque that this portentous event should be linked with an unsuccessful attempt to steal empty bottles. This had been the charge against Martin, alias Dupont.

He returned to his office with card and photograph. The man, in charge of an inspector of police, looked calm and indifferent. Bertillon looked at him.

" I have seen you before. You were arrested last December under the name of Martin; charged with trying to steal empty bottles."

To the prisoner it sounded like the standardized technique to secure an admission, but there was something in the voice of his questioner which vaguely disturbed him.

" No, sir. You are mistaken."

" But I measured you myself. I remember it distinctly."

" You can't put anything on me with measurements. It is the first time I have been here."

" Very well. What about this photograph? Isn't it very like you? Inspector, what do you think of this? Do you see the spot close to the left eyebrow? That is the mole."

The inspector stared. He had been accustomed to look at and to be asked to identify photographs of subjects which for the most part looked as if the pictures had been taken in an inadequately lighted coal-cellar.

" There is no doubt about it, sir. It's very remarkable."

He could not see how these measurements were going to help them, and they interfered with the routine at the Reception Depot; but the photograph impressed him.

The prisoner's voice interrupted this interlude.

" All right. I admit it. And I may as well tell you that my name isn't Martin or Dupont either, in case you guess that too."

Although he had little for such luxuries, Alphonse Bertillon drove off that evening in a fiacre to tell his unofficial secretary the news. He was made to tell the story three or four times and urged to write a note for the papers at once. Characteristically this enthusiasm produced a long lecture on the subject of counting chickens before they were hatched. He wrote to his father, now living at Neuilly, a total invalid and in great pain.

He had to hurry to the Rue Charles-Laffitte where his father lived, for the news of his health was bad. Things seemed not so serious as he had feared, but the truth was that his father had rallied from joy at the good news. One of his aunts was there, his brother Jacques, and two of the Michelet girls. Georges, being in the army, was missing. Compassionate leave did not exist in those days. There was soon a little family celebration in the quiet house by the river. But a few days later there was a sudden dangerous relapse. The doctor's temperature rose steeply, and he was frequently delirious. In the intervals, becoming rapidly shorter, the calm, clear mind survived. It was an abiding comfort that both his adult sons were making their mark in that very field to which he had dedicated his life. It even looked as if the barbarous Alphonse, whose future had worried him so much, might outdistance them all.

He seemed to know precisely when his hour had come and summoned them to his bedside.

" I have always been in search of truth. You, my dear boys, must do the same."

Saying these words, Louis-Adolphe Bertillon died.

13. EXPERIMENTAL EVIDENCE

IT was not in accordance with the Bertillon style to mourn their dead with any outward show of grief. He went back to his work as if nothing had happened, just as his father, to whom he owed so much, would have done. His discovery had been vindicated, and it remained to consolidate the success achieved.

After the initial difficulties of the campaign the success was spectacular. In March of 1883 a second recidivist was identified; in the following quarter, six more. In July, August, and September there were fifteen, and in the last quarter of the year twenty-six. During that year Bertillon made and Amélie Notar recorded 7336 measurements.

During that year also he married his unofficial secretary. It is characteristic of him that there was no formal engagement between them and that the marriage was one of those inevitable events with a statistical certainty of the same order as that which belonged to the anthropometric processes whereby he identified individuals. Probably it had been understood between them for a long time, without any word spoken, that they would ultimately unite.

Perhaps it seemed less inevitable, in the statistical sense, to her than it did to him. Amélie Notar was utterly devoted not only to his interests and work but to the man himself as a person. In her discreet and modest fashion she was determined upon marriage, because any other alternative was simply unthinkable. Even if Bertillon had contemplated remaining single he would have found no defences wherewith to resist pressure of this type.

In this relationship there was dedication to a common purpose, devotion and friendship—but, for his part, no romance at all. This would be remarkable in a man with so strongly romantic a strain if it had not been satisfied elsewhere. As we know, the mystery in Bertillon's life is the secret shrine and the place and function it had in his life and work. Physically the shrine was now far away in Sweden, but for him it was always present and close to his heart. All that he achieved was achieved for the sake of the woman he had placed in it, so that everything could be laid at her feet. If he highly prized, as we know he did, the first honour he was to receive, the Swedish Order, as the earliest recognition of his services to the world he must have done so the more that it was a symbol of her kingdom.

It is perhaps fortunate that he never seems even to have contemplated marriage with this Swedish goddess, and there is no evidence that, given the opportunity, he would have indulged in the fleeting satisfaction of a romantic affair. Had he done so it might well have proved his ruin, for there might have been, with so much energy expended, too little left over for the *magnum opus*. As it worked out, the devotion directed towards the distant shrine returned all the stronger to illuminate and inspire the work.

Certainly such a man was safer with Amélie and her 7336 cards, which otherwise would probably never have been written.

Those cards were to prove very useful immediately in a field beyond the restricted one of criminal identification. What had inspired his father was the proof inherent in the technique that every individual differed from every other. Bertillon was called upon to prove this, not of choice but of necessity. It would be quite a mistake to suppose that his methods of identification were immediately universally accepted. On the contrary, there were many who found it quite impossible to believe that no two human beings could possibly be exactly alike. They had to be answered :

The ideal card of the average man, more exactly the *français banal*, that is to say an individual in whom all the measurements correspond exactly to the average dimensions, quite simply does not exist. It is never found even in the most central section of my cabinets. There are, of course, cards which approach this ideal configuration, but the related measures never approach each other so closely that they can be confused.

These words were spoken in 1893, and behind them was the formidable accumulation of evidence supplied by some 5,000,000 cards; but even at this earlier date Bertillon tenaciously held the conviction of the physical uniqueness of every individual. But the defence quoted was just as necessary in 1893, and later, as it was when his methods were first accepted by the Prefecture of Paris, because, at least in some quarters, scepticism had increased.

Anthropometry is one of the physical sciences, and its theory therefore depends upon experimental evidence for its validity. It is in France that the experimental technique has been most extensively and consistently applied. There is no French example of mistaken identity resulting from the use of Bertillon's methods.

In 1903 an American case occurred which received much publicity at the time. The circumstances were reported to be that an American Negro, named Will West, convicted of an offence, was committed to the prison at Leavenworth, Kansas. On looking through the file, the record-clerk discovered the card of a Will West whose photograph corresponded closely with that of the new prisoner and whose Bertillon measurements were said closely to agree with those found on the card. It was accordingly assumed—although the newly convicted man stoutly denied it—that he had been a previous inmate of that prison. This was proved not to be the fact by the disconcerting discovery that a second Will West, in the flesh and photographically almost indistinguishable from the second prisoner, was actually serving a life-sentence in that very gaol.

The prison governor at that time had recently adopted the fingerprint system of classification. He gave great publicity to the fact that the fingerprints of the two men were quite different. What was not made clear was that the Bertillon measurements of the two men were not identical, although the prison authorities said they were " for practical purposes."

Remarkable in many respects though this coincidence was, the chances that eleven bodily measurements would agree in the same individual are more than four million to one against. These odds are very high. The case did, however, draw attention to a disadvantage of the anthropometric system which the use of fingerprints avoids. They eliminate the necessity of a more or less elaborate system of measurement with its fairly wide margin of error.

In 1883, or in 1893 for that matter, Bertillon's system could not have been subjected to this comparative test, because fingerprints, although discovered, had not been used and approved. Anthropometry continued upon its deservedly triumphant course. Once having adopted the system, the administration seemed to have entertained no doubts as to the soundness of its basis in theory and practice. The steadily accumulating experimental evidence was all in its favour.

The system was still to a large extent ignored by the detective branches of the service. This was due partly to their natural conservatism, and partly to the hostile reaction of Bertillon himself to what he thought was their reactionary attitude. His defects as an expositor either in public or private were notorious, and the department of investigation was perhaps not entirely responsible for its ignorance concerning the anthropometric system and its possibilities in the field of criminal investigation.

They expressed surprise on learning that the dead as well as the living could be identified by this method. More by way of a joke than with any real belief that it would assist the inquiry, he was invited to inspect an unidentified body found afloat on the Marne. It had been in the water some time. The inspector in charge apologized to Bertillon for introducing him to a smelly business. Something in his tone stung the irascible anthropologist.

"You don't realize, inspector, that what you are pleased to call a smelly business may be the last act of justice and mercy at an obscure life's end. But, of course, you wouldn't."

It was a severe reprisal for a minor fault. The inspector reddened and muttered that no offence had been meant.

"None has been taken." But the discomforted inspector got a complete view of the Bertillon back. The neat figure was already at work measuring the wreck of what had once been a man. There was a report soon afterwards from Bertillon's department: Length of the head 200 millimetres, width 163 millimetres, length of middle finger 112 millimetres; elbow joint to middle finger 453 millimetres; height 1.69 metres.

The head was abnormally large in respect of the height, so that the search had been simple. There was a card corresponding to an individual under the name of F——, who had been accused twelve months before of a violent assault. Because of the condition of the body, it had been impossible to record more than five measurements, but, on account of the abnormality observed, the data were thought to be sufficient to establish the identity of the body as that of F——.

It was the man indeed. A case which had looked hopeless was cleared up in a few days. As the result of a violent quarrel concerning a debt two months before the murdered man had been shot and his body thrown into the river. Knowing the identity of the victim, the police had traced his movements and associates at the material time without much difficulty.

Unfortunately, there is no record of the date of this case, but it was certainly prior to the formal establishment of the Department of Judicial Identity in 1888. It is very easy to blame Bertillon's colleagues in the Prefecture for their failure to co-operate with him from the first, but the truth is that they received very little encouragement from the hermit-like specialist who could not meet them on their own ground. Bertillon had an almost pathological horror of publicity, even within the limits of his own professional field, and, by insulating himself in this way, made enemies where he might have found co-operation and support. He also feared being misunderstood when he need not have done so. The results he achieved spoke for themselves.

But even at the height of his success Bertillon remained a square peg in a round hole. The underlying cause was that he would have been a happier man as the pure research worker he would undoubtedly have been, had he become qualified academically and sought the shelter of a university post. He was by temperament unfitted to grapple with practical problems, although by the strength of his character he disciplined himself to do so. He thus suppressed the conflicts of his nature, but never sublimated them. In the result, a characteristically temperamental and irritable man became more temperamental and irritable than ever. None the less, his personal loss was society's gain. Had he worked out his system in a university there is no guarantee that through some proxy it would have taken the practical shape he was obliged to impose upon it, and which, incidentally, made him famous. It is an ironic fact that his defective education was the incidental, if not the direct, cause of his renown.

This defect in the scholastic discipline of thinking, of which he was acutely conscious, made him extremely cautious. Because he was aware of it, Bertillon was able to turn even this to his advantage. He has been represented as a brilliant mathematician, which emphatically he was not. Having little capacity for abstract thinking, he leaned the more heavily upon experimental evidence by which his system stood or fell absolutely. It was partly for this reason that his methods, first adopted in 1882, were not formally recognized until 1888, when the Department of Judicial Identity was formed. By that time the accumulation of experimental evidence was so large that even the initiator of it was convinced that he had created a new branch of science.

It is perhaps a fundamental quality of great men that their weakness and defects, as much as their strength and virtues, somehow conspire together to achieve the desired end. In Bertillon's case this is certainly true. The *élan* of his life, personality, and character was focused upon his work. It bears the indelible imprint of it.

14. THE SPEAKING LIKENESS

WITHIN three or four years the news of Bertillon's discovery had spread throughout France. With his diminutive staff and the help of his wife, whose devotion to the work never flagged, a great mass of evidence concerning the precise description of human individuals had been collected. Herbette, Director of the Penal Administration of the Ministry of the Interior, was considering the adoption of the Bertillon system throughout the prisons of France.

As a result, Bertillon was offered accommodation in the Palais de Justice on the top floor. The rooms were not in a good state of repair. They were badly ventilated, and, being under the roof, they were cold and draughty in winter and extremely hot in summer.

He was prepared to accept this. The trouble began in connexion with the equipment. Willing to endure personal inconvenience, Bertillon insisted that his department must be arranged and equipped so that the work could be efficiently done. In order to save money, the Administration wanted to use unemployed workmen for wages much below those normally paid. It is much to his credit that this produced a typical Bertillon explosion. He was indignant that the Government should try to save a relatively insignificant sum of money by exploiting poverty. In spite of protests which might have jeopardized his future had his superiors not realized that the department and its chief were essential, very little was done to improve the conditions.

Bertillon personally took the matter in hand. By dispensing with supervisory assistance and overseeing the work himself, he was able to conserve the meagre funds at his disposal, and to pay the workmen a fair wage. In two or three days the man who had a reputation for sarcasm and downright rudeness was the idol of the carpenter and plumber's mate. He knew what he wanted; he was always accessible and invariably courteous and considerate. The work was completed in half the time which might have been expended had it been directed by an official " clerk of the works."

On February 1, 1888, Bertillon was installed as Chief of the Service of Judicial Identity. The Prefect of Police presided at the ceremony, and a number of Senators and Deputies were present. Impassive and sardonic, Bertillon sat through the eloquent and lengthy speeches wherein the speakers congratulated him, and yet more themselves for having been the first to recognize the exceptional merits of the young man and his invention.

The material reward was less generous than the sentiments expressed at the installation. Bertillon received a salary of 3600 francs a year (£150). He made no complaint concerning this. As indifferent as any man can be to material considerations, he found it a substantial improvement upon the previous conditions.

Within a month of his appointment Bertillon had recommended that the photographic department should be attached to his. No one in the history of photography did more to destroy the fallacy that the camera never lies than Bertillon. He declared continually that most ordinary photographs of the individual were useless for the purposes of identification. He wanted systematically to introduce the methods of precision which were the basis of anthropometry.

The first and most obvious step was to standardize the photography of the head. It was one of the gravest faults of the classical police photograph that neither the pose nor the lighting conditions was standardized. Bertillon immediately introduced a system whereby a full face and profile portrait appeared upon every identification card.

This innovation in itself fundamentally improved the technique of identification. Quite early in the initiation of the service a certain Xavier Rollin had been measured and photographed. Rollin was a mason and an excellent workman. He was in no sense a criminal, but he had a weakness for strong drink. It made him quarrelsome and brought him into violent collision with his fellow men, occasionally including the police.

On a day in February 1893 he asked leave from his work on account of the illness of one of his relations. He did not return to work next day nor upon the days following. With the passing of the time without news, his wife and family became increasingly anxious. At a period when cinemas did not exist some Parisians were accustomed to amuse themselves by visiting the morgues to view the dead bodies exposed there. On the Sunday following Rollin's disappearance some friends of his had paid a visit to that gruesome place in the quarter of the Ile Saint-Louis. Among the three bodies there they recognized that of their friend Rollin, with the unmistakable moustache and the mocking smile which remained stamped on his features even in death. They immediately went in search of his wife. With tears and lamentations she identified her dead husband.

Bertillon's department photographed the head of the corpse in full face and profile. Every one was struck by the remarkable similarity of both the profile and full face when compared with the photographs upon the police file—every one except Bertillon.

" The same man ! " he snapped. " Look at his right ear ! "

It was conclusive. Neither in size, convolutions, nor in orientation did the ears match. The corpse was that of another man—also, by coincidence, a mason.

The mystery of Rollin's disappearance was solved the next day. He had been in the cells. It was quite true that a relation had been suddenly taken ill, but he had as suddenly recovered. There had been a little celebration. At the close of it Rollin, in a very aggressive frame of mind, recognized an old enemy in a *sergent de ville* who had ventured to tell him that he had better move on. The result of this unfortunate incident was a verdict in the magistrate's court of drunk and disorderly and of assaulting the police; the sentence—seven days' imprisonment.

This case, among scores of others, shows that Bertillon's ideas concerning the importance of precise and detailed photographs were justified. It resulted in the development of a systematized technique which was one of Bertillon's greatest achievements. The *portrait parlé* is a derivative of the anthropometric system. Just as the individual body and limb were measured, so the features were described in terms of small, medium, and large, and measurements were made to particularize the feature in question. But its greatest use is not to identify but to aid recognition, and it survives for this purpose to this day. The sectional photographs were produced by the simple process of making a number of prints of the head in full face and profile and then reducing them to sections, represented, for example, by half the profile, the forehead alone, the forehead including the eyes, the ears, the eyes alone, and the nose alone. These sectional photographs of the same features, but of different individuals, are mounted side by side to show comparison and contrast. It is only when these photographs are seen and studied that we realize how little the polite and casual stare we normally accord our acquaintances tells us about the human face.

It was claimed by Bertillon, and the claim has been amply confirmed since, that if a study of these sectional photographs is made feature by feature the human counterpart can be recognized even if the face has never been seen before. This method of training for the purposes of recognition, as distinct from formal identification, was introduced by him. It was a great success. Police recruits, as well as the higher ranks, showed great interest in this new kind of photographic album.

One of the difficulties arising in connexion with photography was the resistance offered by the subjects to being photographed at all. It is a remarkable fact that Bertillon personally appears to have had little difficulty on this score. He never resorted to threats or force and always treated his subjects with courtesy. His experience was in contrast to that of the New York detective organization which adopted his methods very soon after the formation of Bertillon's department in France. There is a most interesting contemporary sketch showing the photographing of a subject for the American Rogue's Gallery. He is being held by four men, and appears to be making a violent resistance. This sketch serves to remind us of the technical difficulties of this kind of photography at a period when long time-exposures were the rule and the command " Now quite still, please " had to be obeyed to the letter.

There are, of course, other ways of trying to defeat the ends of photographic justice. In November 1883, when the new method of photography in full face and profile had not long been introduced, a boy named Raoul was arrested for some minor offence. He made no resistance to being photographed, and he obeyed the photographer's instructions. Six months later the youth, now calling himself Billardo, was again arrested. Raoul had learnt something of the tricks of the trade. The superficial appearance of a boy of seventeen can change in six months. He had accentuated the alteration by adopting a different style of hair-cut. There was again no active resistance to being photographed, but instead of looking into the lens of the camera he turned his eyes to look at the photographer, who stood on the right of his apparatus. He grimaced a little, mockingly. A comparison of the two photographs in full face is a striking illustration of that experience common to all of us when we say or think that " we have seen that face before." It is, in fact, an assertion of doubt rather than certainty.

The profile portrait tells a more convincing story. ' Expression,' that pitfall of identification, is neutralized, but the structure and pattern of the features shown by both photographs correspond so closely that they put the probability of identity very high. The subject is recognizable.

This does not alter the fact that neither Bertillon's measurements nor his photography sufficed to identify the young with judicial certainty. The measurements always, the individual marks of identity and the recognizable structure of the face sometimes, change between childhood, adolescence, and adult life. None the less, his measurements, even of the young, and his *portrait parlé* represent a system which was a spectacular advance upon anything achieved before in this field. This is true in particular of his technical photography as an aid to recognition.

It has been claimed that the photographing of criminals was first initiated in the '30's of the last century. This is less historically important than the fact that in 1883 France was the only country in the world where photographs having a real significance as a means of identification were being taken as a matter of routine.

The new photographic technique was soon to be applied in other fields. It was the beginning of the applied science of criminal investigation which is called in French *criminalistique* and in English forensic science. Bertillon was no theoretician or abstract thinker, but he had the faculty of being able to apply all the knowledge he had to practical and useful ends, and to apply it always to the best advantage. Others could speculate concerning the definitions and principles of scientific evidence. He was concerned with the precise measurement of the human being and with taking exact photographs which, in their essentials, meant the same thing for every one. This was the reason for his spectacular success and for the fact that his name was soon known throughout Europe and the United States. For the police, who are concerned with the difficult and responsible task of detecting and trying to prevent crime, theoretical science is of no interest at all. They can be impressed by science and technology only in the result. Bertillon had given them results.

The next, and perfectly logical, step was the development of metric photography. Bertillon introduced a measuring scale, with the object photographed so that there was a permanent record of the scale of the photograph in general. This scale could also actually be used to measure any flat surface which was at right angles to the lens and in the same plane as the scale. As the result of this development, he went with his photographic apparatus to the scenes of many crimes to record the position of the body and its relation to the surrounding objects in cases of murder, and to produce photographs of windows and doors showing their size and the nature and extent of the damage in affairs of housebreaking, the position, size, and shape of footprints, stains, and other *corpus delicti* which are so often vital clues in the solution of a crime. Before his application of precision photography to criminal investigation, these things had to be sketched with varying degrees of precision or simply described, often without any precision at all.

This was to apply his basic methods of identification to the clue as well as to the person. In the modern technique of criminal investigation, which he, in everyday practice initiated, a speaking likeness is required not only of the person, but of the objects and traces, whether great or small, which he leaves behind him on the scene of his felony or misdemeanour. These specialized matters had a resounding impact which extended far beyond their apparently restricted field. Like many people who have justly won renown, Bertillon has often been praised and blamed for the wrong reasons. He has been praised as the initiator of the system of identification by fingerprints. It is a distinction to which he is not entitled and which he never claimed. He has been savagely attacked for his part in the Dreyfus Affair upon the wrong grounds by men, many of whom reviled him less in the cause of justice than from motives of political or personal dislike.

It is in relation to a much wider background that scientific history ought to judge him. His real achievement was that he was one of the creators of criminal investigation as an applied science, and he was thus one of the architects of the modern concepts of justice. This is an ethical question. Because of the highly developed moral qualities of the man, the essential drive behind all his work was an ethical one. There were times when he bored his listeners with dissertations which suggested only that he worshipped precision to the point of idolatry; but, in the result, his anthropometry and everything else that he did was part of the master plan to overthrow the corrupt system of guesswork which preceded it. It had its effect. Among detectives fact-finding as an aid to criminal inquiry began seriously to compete with the hearsay evidence of the informer and the stool-pigeon. This was not founded upon sudden conversion or change of heart, but upon the accumulating evidence that these new methods were often more efficient as well as more cleanly than the old.

Even if he realized it he would have been too wary to admit that his success was as much a moral as a scientific one. But when the defensive façade of the calculating man of science wore thin, as it occasionally did, the essential humanism of his approach even to all professional problems came diffidently through. It was perhaps for this reason that under-dogs, many of them with very bad names, with whom he had to deal professionally never seemed particularly to resent, even if they feared, the new scientific ' once over ' of which Bertillon was the master and to which they had to submit according to law. The whole experience of being ' identified ' had changed under the new system. If more awe-inspiring than the old-fashioned method, even the most hardened recognized that it was more just. However much the criminal man may have feared the precise photograph and the exact measurement, it is unlikely that they suspected the man who did these strange things of manipulating to their disadvantage the figures he so carefully wrote down.

Apart from the revolution he brought about in technique, it was the new habit of mind which Bertillon brought to police methods which is so significant. It was not only a scientific revolution which he initiated : it was a legal and social one.

15. M. ALAUX'S CABINET

IT was October 17, 1902. The telephone-bell rang in Bertillon's office. An impatient voice asked for him. The caller was not to be put off by the gambit that the Chief of the Department was busy and could a message be left.

" Of course he is busy," the voice snapped; " but it is Joliot, examining magistrate. I must speak to M. Bertillon immediately."

Bertillon came to the telephone and listened to the thin, sharp voice, interrupted by cracklings inseparable from all telephones, and particularly French ones, in those days.

" Serious trouble in the Faubourg Saint-Honoré—murder. Come to my office at once and bring your photographer with you if you can."

Bertillon never liked the field-work. He loved his work of classification and its theory and technique. When it came to him in his office he was devoted to the photography of the human face and body; but he preferred the living subject to the corpse, and his instinct was to retreat before the disordered apparatus of murder with its blood and confusion.

But soon afterwards he, with Joliot, Sorquet, the medico-legist, and Cochefer, a Departmental Chief of the Sûreté, were at 157 Rue du Faubourg Saint-Honoré. It was a handsome and luxuriously furnished flat, maintained by a fashionable surgeon-dentist named Alaux. The surgery and office formed part of the suite.

An office called the ' cashier's room ' was in disorder. A desk and a glass cabinet had been broken open. Chairs and other furniture had been overturned and broken. In the midst of this confusion was a body sitting with its back resting against a chair with the legs extended. The end of the victim's shirt had been pulled from beneath the trousers. Dark and swollen though the face was, with cyanosed lips and protruding eyes, it was recognizable as that of Joseph Reibel, the dentist's valet.

The surgeon knelt down beside the body and closely examined the neck.

"Strangled!" he said. "Manually, I should think. The post-mortem will clear that up."

He studied the swollen face in detail.

"Plenty for you to photograph here, M. Bertillon. You see those marks on the face?"

Bertillon looked at the skin with distaste, but closely. "Finger-nails," he said.

The doctor nodded. "Yes, you are right."

In the background the superintendent was examining the furniture, and grumbling.

"Something wrong here. Desk and cabinet forced, and yet there has been very little taken. Keys on the mantelpiece, too."

Alphonse Bertillon went over everything in his slow methodical fashion. The camera was set up and the paper-scales, accurately marked in indian ink, placed in position so that the objects photographed could be shown in their size to scale. They stood by to take. The room was suddenly illuminated with the cold and ghastly brilliance of burning magnesium ribbon. He photographed the body exactly as it lay, and then brought the camera nearer for a close-up of the injuries and marks upon the face.

They watched him, fascinated. Photography was then still something of a new toy to the police. They had no experience of using cameras as Bertillon used them, and remained sceptical of the need for recording all this detail and incorporating measurement with it.

The drawing-room was less disordered, but a half-hearted attempt had been made to rifle it. One of the glass panels of a cabinet containing *objets d'art* had been broken, and there were a few vacant places upon the shelves. The superintendent continued to grumble. It was not a simple burglary. It looked all wrong.

He was bending over pieces of broken glass fallen from the

cabinet. They were stained with blood. When he was about to pick one of the pieces up Bertillon, with unaccustomed haste, darted to his side and held his arm.

"Don't touch that," he snapped; "don't touch it."

The superintendent resented this peremptory command. He was met with one of Bertillon's unexpectedly disarming smiles.

"You must excuse the zeal of a photographer, superintendent."

"Just so, sir," the superintendent spoke a little stiffly; "but why?"

Bertillon produced an immaculate pocket-handkerchief. It looked alien against the background of blood, broken glass, and confusion. Very carefully he picked up a large fragment using the handkerchief to shield his fingers from contact with the surface. He held the glass up to the light.

"You see those?" He pointed to a number of small blood-stained marks.

"Yes, sir—fingerprints."

"As you say, fingerprints! I must photograph them. If you had handled this with uncovered hands you might have destroyed the evidence."

"But are they any good, sir?"

"I don't know," said Bertillon; "but we can try."

At that time fingerprint evidence was not regarded with much favour in Paris. Ordinary detectives did not understand the system and were very sceptical concerning it. The superintendent probably watched with some impatience the slow and methodical care with which Bertillon himself packed his precious exhibits so that their surfaces should not be chafed and the stains upon them altered or effaced.

Bertillon's scepticism was of a different order from theirs. He believed in testing everything. He had an almost Teutonic thoroughness and preoccupation with detail.

In the meantime the investigation went on. It was not a simple one. There was a good deal of nervousness in this fashionable and wealthy neighbourhood, and some criticism of the police when arrests were not made immediately. If housebreakers could enter apartments by force, murder occupants, and escape without difficulty with their loot, no one was

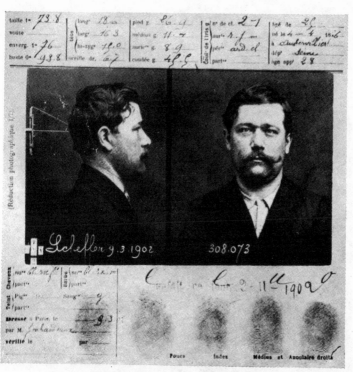

BERTILLON'S PHOTOGRAPH OF HENRI-LÉON SCHEFFER
Scheffer was the first man in Europe to be convicted on
fingerprint evidence alone.

THE CARTOON FROM "L'ASSIETTE AU BEURRE,"
SAID TO REFER TO THE SCHEFFER CASE

[*See pp.* 117–118.]

safe. The critics did not know that the crime was not as straightforward as this. All suspects who might have been supposed to have committed a crime of this kind were either in prison or could account for their movements. That this was no ordinary burglary was shown by the simple fact that there had been no forcible entry. It also appeared that the violence used upon the desk and cabinet was artificial and intended to suggest that robbery had been the motive of the crime. One thousand six hundred francs had disappeared and a few silver ornaments among a large and valuable collection. If robbery were the only motive the police thought the stakes should have been higher and the technique more systematic since the thief was prepared to risk committing murder.

There were hurried and anxious conferences. The dentist was interrogated, and, although clearly in no way implicated, he was in certain respects an unwilling witness. M. Alaux evidently suspected his valet of being a homosexual. Reibel had been associating with a man who, he said, was a relation and who had visited him at the apartment. He was known only under the name of Georges. The dentist suspected, although he could not prove, that there was a sexual association between the two men. This was perhaps the real motive of the murder.

For some days they made no progress at all. But on October 24 Joliot received a report from Bertillon which, as he said, " flashed a sudden light upon the mystery."

Bertillon had gone to work systematically upon his exhibits, and had produced photographs of the bloodstained fingerprints which compared favourably with the best examples of forensic photography to-day. At that time photographic equipment was not what it is at the present time. Infra-red and ultra-violet photography were unknown; colour sensitive plates were little used; and illumination apparatus was comparatively rudimentary. It was not a simple matter to produce actual photographs of brown smudges upon a glass surface. In his meticulous fashion he noted down all the methods he had used to secure these photographs, whether they were successful or not. By this patient process of trial and error he found that the best results were given by photographing the surface against a black background using a powerful arc-lamp placed close to the camera lens with the rays directed almost vertically upon the object.

This method produced clear pictures of four finger-marks belonging to a thumb, an index, a middle, and a ring finger with three, four, four, and six points of resemblance respectively.

The search began. It was laborious and involved many hours of patient work. Bertillon's scepticism concerning fingerprints for a long time discouraged him from including them upon his anthropometric cards. Since 1900 he had done so, but he had not allowed them to interfere with his anthropometric system of classification. The result of this was that he had not at that time, and never in fact had at any future time, a satisfactory system of fingerprint classification.

Fortunately for him, there were not yet on the files the vast collection of fingerprints which exist in any large bureau now. None the less, there were before him and his assistants two or three days of heavy work which might well have been all in vain. There was no good reason to believe that this killer had been in the hands of the police before. On the contrary, if this were a pervert's crime it was likely enough that the author had never previously been convicted.

He must have felt something of that elation which had almost overwhelmed him in 1883 when they found the card. This was as great an occasion as when Martin, alias Dupont, had been recognized as the man who had once been convicted of pilfering empty milk-bottles. Henri Léon Scheffer, born April 4, 1876, thumb—loop, index—loop, middle—loop approximating arch, ring—whorl. These designs agreed with those found on the broken glass in the Rue du Faubourg Saint-Honoré. They set to work to check the prints in detail.

It was the report resulting from this discovery which threw (as Joliot said) " a flash of light upon the mystery." The date of it was October 24, 1902.

On the 17th of this month I was instructed by M. Joliot, examining magistrate, to photograph the apartment situated at 157 Rue du Faubourg Saint-Honoré, where a crime had been committed upon the person of a certain Reibel, servant in the service of M. Alaux, dentist.

This work led me to reproduce some finger impressions clearly shown upon a sheet of glass in M. Alaux's drawing-room. . . .

A Bertillon report never left anything to the imagination. It goes on to explain that these prints must have been left either by the supposed murderer, by his victim, or by some other person who had entered the apartment, and, since it was impossible to verify the last hypothesis, the writer had confined himself to the first two. In the process of verifying these, it had been possible at once to eliminate the fingerprints of the victim, because the prints found did not agree in any respect with those of Reibel.

Even his genius for understatement could not suppress a hint of the painful process of the search. It remained only to make a most careful search of the anthropometric records, where a card was found concerning a certain Henri Léon Scheffer. (Effectuées avec le plus grand soin, elles ont fait découvrir une fiche concernant un nommé Scheffer, Henri Léon, âgé de 26 ans . . . dont les empreintes digitales concordent, d'une manière frappante, avec celles relevées sur le lieu du crime.)

His excellent photographs are included, showing the manner whereby he had isolated three points of resemblance in the thumb-print, four in the index and middle finger, and six in the ring finger. The loops he calls *lacets* (now called *boucles*), and he rightly described the pattern of the middle finger as a loop approximating an arch, indicating that he must have been familiar with and have accepted Henry's nomenclature, although he does not use his formal descriptions. (Pour le Médius, sillons en forme d'arcs superposés avec, au centre de l'empreinte, un seul lacet oblique à droite renfermant un sillon central.)

He then minutely describes the points of resemblance for the benefit of his colleagues, who were but slightly acquainted with the technique of fingerprint identification. In order to clarify the matter further he adopted a method of demonstration which he retained throughout his life. This was to outline carefully with very fine ink-strokes the points of resemblance found so that their design stood out in relief against a background which is very confusing to the untutored eye.

The search for Reibel's murderer could begin in earnest. A dental mechanic immediately recognized the photograph as greatly resembling the mysterious "Georges." Although his last conviction had been for fraud and robbery, *la police des mœurs* recognized the portrait of Scheffer as a man they had had under observation for some time. Having thus identified him, correspondence addressed to him in Paris was watched and intercepted. Scheffer was traced to Marseilles.

I am indebted to Dr Sannié, Director of the Natural History Museum and Chief of the Service of Judicial Indentity of the Prefecture of Police, for the facts upon which this account of the Scheffer case is founded. It is probably the most significant in the European history of fingerprints. On this evidence it is not possible to deprive Bertillon of the merit of being the first expert in Europe to effect the solution of a murder investigation upon fingerprint evidence alone. The conclusion of this affair was that, at the end of his resources, Scheffer gave himself up to the police of Marseilles and confessed his crime. It is thus, of course, technically quite true that Scheffer might have been convicted without the fingerprint evidence, because he threw himself upon the mercy of the law. On the other hand, by reason of that evidence, the police were already in search of him, and his surrender anticipated them only by a very short period of time. This does not affect the ultimate conclusion concerning the unique character of the convicting evidence. As far as is known, there were no facts, discovered then or later, other than his own confession, whereby he could have been convicted. The evidence of visual identity was uncertain. There was no one to say that he, or anyone resembling him, had been seen in or near M. Alaux's apartment at the material time. It does not appear that any of the stolen property was ever traced to him.

In this connexion there is one detail of this singular case which remains unexplained. If Scheffer was thief as well as murderer he was in possession of about £80 on October 17. On or about October 27, ten days later, he was at the end of his resources. Even allowing for the well-known prodigality of the criminal and particularly those who commit crimes of violence, it seems a high rate of expenditure of money with the value it then had.

There is nothing to show that this spectacular success greatly increased Bertillon's confidence in fingerprint identification. The complete text of his report will be found in Appendix III. Commenting upon it and upon Bertillon's photographs, Dr Sannié has observed that he could have shown many more points of resemblance in the traces he found had he been more fully acquainted with fingerprint technique. The Bertillon report is a bare statement of fact. It is not suggested anywhere that the fingerprint evidence is a complete proof of identity. The resemblance between the traces found on the scene of the crime and the prints of the suspect is ' striking,' but this does not commit the author of this significant document to the view that Scheffer must be their man and none other.

Curiously enough, this case did not attract much public attention at the time. It was later that it became part of the legend that Bertillon was the father of fingerprint science. The opinion was most embarrassing to him, and the more so because it was made the subject of a good deal of facetious comment in Parisian illustrated papers.

The misfortunes of the Dreyfus Affair had much increased the great man's horror of publicity. It was now almost a pathological dread. Also, in spite of his pointed and malicious wit, he was in certain respects deficient in a sense of humour. He could see nothing amusing in a caricature which appeared in about 1910 depicting him upon a scaffolding demolishing the wall of a building for the purpose of being able to preserve a fingerprint upon a single brick. It was a good-humoured piece of work and would have been quite inoffensive to anyone of normal sensitivity. Perhaps he had more reason to resent a cartoon which appeared in *L'Assiette au Beurre* on July 3, 1909, which is said to refer to the Scheffer case. Immaculately dressed and wearing his top hat, Bertillon is represented in a primitive W.C. examining finger-marks on the wall—apparently produced with material which might be expected to be found there—by the light of a candle. In order that nothing may be left to the imagination, the caption puts these words into Bertillon's mouth—"*Un assassin laisse toujours des traces ' quelque part.'*" There may, of course, have been a trace of malice in the mind of the artist, a man who called himself Musacchio, but it is more probable that it was a typical example of that good-humoured grossness which is better tolerated in Paris than in London.

It was not, however, tolerated by him. He was not one of those men who reacted well to the theory that the pinnacles of fame have been reached when a man is caricatured in the newspapers. None the less, whether he liked it or not, it was a symptom of the regard in which he was held as much by the man in the street as by his scientific and more intellectual colleagues.

Apart from its significance in the history of identification, his field-work established once and for all the great significance of the technical approach to the problem of criminal investigation. The reputation won by the French police at the beginning of this century was not solely due to Bertillon's work in Paris, but he made as large a contribution to it as any man of his time. On a last analysis the affair of M. Alaux's cabinet is significant, not because it discloses Bertillon as fully abreast or ahead of his time in the latest identification technique, but because it illustrates his high competence as a technologist, and his objective approach to investigational problems, two essential things without which the science of criminal investigation cannot exist.

16. THE CRIME LABORATORY

THE crime laboratory is something which is now accepted as a necessary element in the work of criminal investigation. Every policeman on the beat knows that the technical work of the laboratory may help in the solution of almost every kind of crime, and that one branch of science or another can in many cases supply indisputable proof of the innocence or guilt of an accused or suspected person. In the investigation of a crime, while nothing can replace the patient routine work which the police have to do in the field, they have long recognized what scientific aid can do for them.

It was very different in the late nineteenth century when Bertillon and his friends began to achieve their successes. The debt which posterity owes to Bertillon is not only on account of his discovery of the first systematic means of identifying the person. It is the principle behind it which is so vitally significant. This was the scientific approach to every problem of crime, the solution of those questions posed by the unnamed Roman jurist who asked:

> What was the crime? Who did it?
> When was it done, and where?
> How done, and with what motive?
> Who in the deed did share?

Bertillon, who was reticent by nature, was extremely so concerning his laboratory work, so that the results of it have to be reconstructed from material which it would be more easy to interpret if he had published more concerning it and if he had publicized his achievement. Despite this, it is possible to produce a picture in outline of his research in the field of police technology.

It was in this workshop that he was most at home. One

section of it was devoted to experimental methods of recording traces found upon the scene of the crime. Bertillon did not devise the method of making plaster-casts of footprints and other impressions, but he was the first to develop a practical method of producing a metallic replica of a plaster-cast so as to produce a permanent record of the impression. The method was essentially to coat the plaster surface with graphite so that it would conduct an electric current and then electrically to deposit metallic copper upon the graphited surface. A metallic replica, exact in every detail, was thus produced from the plaster-cast.

This was, in principle, an inevitable development of his photographic methods of record. A good photograph is a record for all time; so also is a metallic casting of a fragile plaster mould.

It was for the same reason that Bertillon became absorbed with experiments in connexion with the development of fingerprints. If a fingerprint is to be made a permanent record it has to be associated with some imperishable material, such as a mineral powder in a sufficiently fine state of division for the particles to adhere to the greasy surface of the ridge markings, thus not only making them visible but fixing them permanently as a record of the individual who had produced them.

Perhaps as early as 1896 he could have been seen absorbed in his experiments with finely powdered graphite, which was the first substance he used for the development of latent finger impressions. Bertillon applied the material with a soft camelhair brush, which was also used to remove the excess of the powder. For many years this reagent was accepted as a standard developer of fingerprints in France.

It was not until later that he discovered the value of the heavier powders as developers, but the principle and practice of the development of fingerprints with the oxides and carbonate of lead are due to him, and it is to him we owe the discovery of red lead as a developer which is still often used to-day.

He did not personally favour the use of chemical methods of development, perhaps because he was not well acquainted with chemical theory and practice; but Bertillon closely followed the investigations of Forgeot and his colleagues in Lyon. Although this is not generally recognized, Forgeot devised one of the most remarkable methods of finger-print development. In quite a different connexion Forgeot had discovered that perspiration reacted with silver nitrate to pro-duce a black compound after exposure to light. He later utilized this method to develop invisible fingerprints on paper. His method has since been developed and utilized for the treatment of latent fingerprints upon surfaces upon which other developers cannot be used, such as textile fabrics and unglazed wood.

Bertillon was more at home with instruments than with chemical reagents. He was justly proud of his improvements in the design of photographic equipment, but he cherished even more the mechanical contrivances which he devised to aid the detective in his work. Curiously enough, the invention which he prized above all was his dynamometer, a costly and complicated piece of apparatus designed to measure the force applied by the housebreaker in using his tools. Essentially this instrument consisted of two steel test-plates, one of which was rigid while the other could be adjusted to move against the tension of a spring which was connected with a dynamometer. The method of using the instrument was to insert a piece of wood between two test-plates and then to insert the appro-priate tool between the wood and the mobile plate. The tool was then forced against the wood to produce an impression similar to that of the damaged wood found upon the scene of the crime. The force used transferred to the mobile test-plate was registered upon the dynamometer in terms of pres-sure in kilogrammes.

It is doubtful if this ingenious and formidable apparatus was much used in practice, and, if it were, that the results were of much help in the ordinary practice of criminal investiga-tion. The generally accepted opinion was that if the police could trace and secure the housebreaker the amount of force he had used in effecting an entry was of very little importance.

This academic interest in the problems of criminal investi-gation was none the less an essential element of Bertillon's versatile mind. He had a reverence for facts and figures and a drive to pursue the abstract as well as the concrete aspect of any problem.

But even the dynamometer was less of a white elephant than its critics supposed. Its use encouraged the study of the marks and impressions made by housebreaking implements, of which Bertillon made an intensive study. It had many applications in everyday practice.

In a case of burglary which involved the breaking of a roll-top desk, M. Albanel, the examining magistrate in charge of the case, invited Bertillon to attend at the scene of the crime, an apartment in the Rue de la Pépinière, to reconstruct the method whereby the locked desk had been forced.

The room was in confusion, but the centre of attention was the rifled desk, of which the lock had been clumsily forced. The examining magistrate wanted to know what implements had been used to effect the breakage and, if more than one had been employed, in what order they had been applied to break open the desk. He was discussing the matter with the superintendent and his assistant. It was a theoretical and speculative discussion. Bertillon remained silent. He was asked his opinion and refused to offer one.

" What is the use of an opinion without facts? Send the desk round to my laboratory, and I will see what can be done."

The examining magistrate still wanted an opinion on the spot, but his determination broke against Bertillon's cold obstinacy. It was a laboratory examination or nothing. M. Albanel shrugged his shoulders and gave in with the best grace he could.

There were two suspects, named Renard and Courtois. The police had seized certain implements which they believed had been used to break open the bureau—a metal punch and two chisels. Bertillon shut himself up in his laboratory with the *corpus delicti* and set to work.

The result was one of those long, arid, and detailed reports for which the great man had become famous. Bertillon never solved the problem of condensation. Everything must be put down, and every conclusion, however obvious, had to be set out to the last and most trivial detail. Yet this report is a classic of its kind. It is a prototype wherein are included the essential principles and methods of criminal investigation as it is understood to-day, the canon of the experimental method.

A, the first chisel, B, the second chisel, and C, the punch, represent three groups. Each group can give rise to two combinations according to the order in which the other two implements are used in conjunction with the first.

Group I Chisel A	Chisel B, Punch (1)
	Punch, Chisel B (2)
Group II Chisel B	Chisel A, Punch (3)
	Punch, Chisel A (4)
Group III Punch	Chisel A, Chisel B (5)
	Chisel B, Chisel A (6)

The order shown by Group I (1 and 2) was at once eliminated, because it was found that chisel A was too thick to have been used for the preliminary attack. This tool was broken, but the breakage had not occurred as a result of the forcing of the desk. The broken surface was rusty.

Group II (3 and 4) was also eliminated but for a different reason. The operative surface of the tool was carefully measured. Impressions made by it using different degrees of force as registered by the dynamometer did not correspond with those found on the desk. The impressions were too deep and could only have been produced if a hammer had been used to drive the implement home. There was no hammer.

Group III (5 and 6) thus determined which implement had first been used to break open the desk—namely, the punch.

The experiments were repeated with this to discover the nature and dimensions of the marks made with it using varying degrees of force. These experimental marks when made by levering the punch up and down agreed with those found on the rifled desk.

Which implement was next used? On the right of the desk lock Bertillon found marks corresponding to those of chisel B. They were of a depth and size which showed from the dynamometric reading that considerable force had been used, and that the implement had been inserted not at right angles to the desk lid but obliquely. Having to some extent loosened the desk lid with the punch, the thinner instrument which could not effectively have been used before had been brought into operation. The fact that considerable force had been used indicated that its work had been done at an intermediate stage.

Chisel A had been used only at the final stage when the space between the desk lid and the side was sufficiently large to introduce it. Less force had been applied because the operation of forcing the lid was already far advanced.

The order in which the instruments had been used was thus established. First the punch, second chisel B, and third chisel A.

The report then goes on to argue at some length whether this order of instrumentation was compatible with the manipulations of one operator, or whether more than one must have been engaged upon the work. Dismissing as inadequate the commonsense conclusion that no man in his senses, having found an instrument adapted to his purpose, would employ two others merely for the sake of using them, an inductive proof is brought to bear upon the problem.

Not only the order in which the instruments had been used, but the disposition of the impressions showed that at least two men must have been at work upon the desk. This was confirmed by the fact that, although upon castors, there were no traces upon the floor of any appreciable movement of the desk. The inference was that the assistant, while operating the subsidiary tool as a lever, had also held the desk firmly so that his principal could work efficiently upon the lid and lock.

An impatient examining magistrate had to wait until the lengthy and detailed report was finished. But at least it told him what he wanted to know. Bertillon did not know the details of the statement made by the suspect Courtois. In his first statement he had admitted that Renard had helped him to break open the desk, and they had used the tools in the order and in the manner described by Bertillon in his report. He had been asked to make the examination, because Courtois had subsequently withdrawn his statement and declared that his accomplice, who had denied participation, had not been concerned with the desk-breaking.

Hundreds of such cases occur every year and have to be

dealt with by the police as a matter of routine. They have no sensational aspect and are about as far removed from the *cause célèbre* as any crime could be. None the less, it was the fate of these two petty malefactors to share in the making of the history of criminal investigation. This quite insignificant affair, from the point of view of crime committed, is one of the landmarks in the development of the technique of ' the reconstruction of the crime.' This phrase is now very well known; but its classical meaning was quite different from its modern equivalent, and it had a sinister reputation and history which was not ill-deserved. The investigators, having made a speculative build-up of the mechanics of the crime, re-enacted it in the presence of the suspect, the theory being that if the reconstruction was accurate a confession or admission would automatically follow. As well as being psychologically unsound, the method was open to the grossest abuse by association with the methods of the third degree.

Bertillon was in the vanguard with the pioneers who created a new method of scientific, as distinct from speculative, reconstruction whereby the mechanics of the crime were built up upon a factual basis. Where there were no facts, there could be no reconstruction. Just as his scientific technique of identification had lifted the whole problem out of the region of guesswork, so the principles applied to this quite minor case were, in fact, the foundations of a new pattern and structure in criminal investigation. It is, in fact, all the more significant that he gave as much time and energy to this affair as he would have given had it been some notorious murder-case. For him the quality of the crime was of no importance. His great discovery in the field of identification had been linked with a theft of empty milk-bottles. This did not minimize its vital significance as a new stage in the evolution of scientific method.

II

It was not until later that the laboratory became concerned with the scientific examination of documents. Bertillon's greatest technical skill had always been focused upon photography, because of its essential connexion with his anthropometric work. As a result of his reputation as a photographer, his services were utilized to photograph not only criminals and the scenes of their crimes, but miscellaneous objects of which accurate records were required. The practical value of photography as a means of copying documents was beginning to be recognized towards the end of the nineteenth century. With increasing frequency Bertillon's department was called upon to do work of this kind.

He was among the first to recognize the value of contact photography without the use of a camera for the photographic reproduction of certain types of document.

In the *Revue Scientifique* of April 1889 he was writing enthusiastically of the uses of contact photography for the reproduction of admitted and questioned documents. Nothing, he said, was more simple than to place the document in intimate contact with a photographic plate and to expose it for a few seconds to the light of a gas-jet. By this means not only was the writing produced in natural size, but since the light was transmitted through the paper its fibrous structure was very clearly defined. This method also clearly exposed any variation in thickness of the paper. He had been able to show the existence of very careful erasures upon questioned documents by this method when they were not readily visible by ordinary inspection.

These photographic experiments stimulated his interest in the examinations of documents generally. To Bertillon we owe the discovery of what is known as the phenomenon of ink-discharge. This is the property possessed by certain ink writings to leave a latent image of the writing upon the plain surface of a piece of paper with which the writing has been in contact. This latent impression can be developed and has been effectively used to detect certain kinds of manipulative forgery. If a document has been folded in such a way that part of its plain surface has been in contact with the written matter the discharged image (in reverse) may be produced and may be capable of development. In cases where words or figures have been fraudulently deleted from the document after this discharge has taken place the fraud has been shown as a fact by development of the latent image. This, of course, includes the original words or figures which have been removed.

Bertillon thought that this discharge was due to the transference of the gummy material of the ink to the surface of the contacting paper. It was afterwards shown by his pupil Reiss that the discharge is, in fact, due to certain acid constituents of the ink. He developed contact methods of photography, first suggested by Bertillon, to make the latent ' mirror writing ' visible.

Reiss is justly renowned as one of the pioneers in application of photography to criminal investigation. His book *La Photographie Judiciaire* is everywhere recognized as a classic; but Reiss was the first to admit his debt to Bertillon, who was indisputably the creator of the first principles and practice of judicial photography.

It is not surprising that it should have been his favourite method for the investigation of the questioned document as it was of the suspect person. To-day, with the vast progress made in the manufacture of optical instruments and, in particular, the camera and its illumination equipment, it is not easy to realize the difficulties of the nineteenth-century worker in this field. The most satisfactory source of artificial illumination was the carbon arc-lamp which Bertillon did much to improve. Infra-red and ultra-violet photography were unknown (see Appendix VI). The only form of flash-light illumination was the magnesium ribbon. Yet with his rudimentary apparatus Bertillon was able to produce remarkable results. He could photograph faint traces of pen-marks of erased writing directly enlarged four diameters which were almost invisible under ordinary inspection using his carbon arc as a source, or even, in some cases, bright sunlight. He had no panchromatic plates, but he developed the use of coloured filters, which he made indispensable to efficient document photography.

As a result of these activities, he was presently to be faced with the problem of handwriting itself. It is a legend that Bertillon ever professed to be a handwriting expert. On the contrary, he dogmatically asserted that it was impossible to identify the person by means of his handwriting. What he did

was to apply to handwriting the methods of comparison used
in his anthropometric system.

Photographs of the document were cut up, word by word,
and stuck upon cards vertically in alphabetical order, the
words of the questioned and admitted writings being arranged
alternately. An additional set of words were mounted individually on filing-cards, those of the disputed writings being red
and those of the admitted writings blue. This facilitated the
rapid juxtaposing of any two cards representing admitted and
questioned writings possessing like words or like groups of
letters, and their comparison.

·This classified photographic service was utilized by those
who were concerned with the examination of questioned
writings. Documents were continually being submitted to
Bertillon's department for photographing and sectionalizing
by this method. After ten years a very large number of these
sectional photographs had been accumulated. In 1898
Bertillon made his system the subject of a paper published in
the *Revue Scientifique—La Comparaison des Ecritures e*
l'Identification Graphique. It was a cautious exposition of
the object of the classification which was to facilitate the
comparison of any two or more given pieces of writing
Bertillon never implied that writings could be positively
identified by this method.

This is of great significance in the history of Bertillon's life
and work and to the history of handwriting expertise. I
throws light, as shall presently be found, upon the problem
of the notorious Dreyfus case and helps to explain how
Bertillon came to be involved in it and the real nature of his
error in the interpretation of· the evidence.

It would be to anticipate to pursue that matter at this stage
What we are here concerned with is the fact that Bertillon'
laboratory work and his creation of a technical department
for the investigation of crime were the beginning of a new era
in criminal investigation. Up to that time science had played
no part in detection, except in the field of legal medicine. He
was one of the creators of the crime laboratory, and the
example he had set in Paris was soon to be followed elsewhere
His friend Lacassagne founded his laboratory in Lyon, where

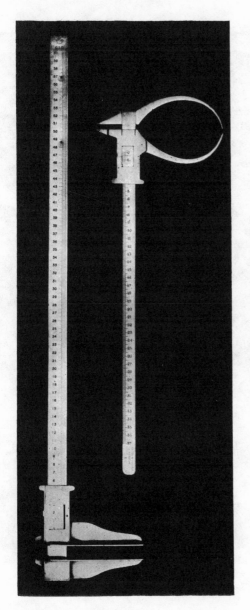

TWO OF BERTILLON'S MEASURING INSTRUMENTS

THE SINKING OF THE "DRUMMOND CASTLE"
From the *Illustrated London News*.

they studied fingerprints and dusts, and submitted to scientific scrutiny every kind of object found on the scene of a crime. Very little progress was made at first, and the obstruction which Bertillon suffered was even more pronounced in the less important prefectures. None the less, they were ultimately to succeed, and much of their achievement was due to the inspiration of the man who had first discovered a scientific means of identifying the person.

17. THE "DRUMMOND CASTLE" TRAGEDY

IT was three o'clock in the morning of June 17, 1896. The weather was thick with small rain. There was a strong south-westerly wind and a considerable sea running. Before dawn two Breton fishermen who had been trawling in the Fromveur Sound, off Ushant, thought they heard a cry for help. They were not certain of this, but they cruised about for a considerable time until it was quite light. The fishermen found nothing, and concluded that they must have been mistaken.

In fact, it is probable that they were not. At midnight not far from where they were one of the worst maritime disasters of the century had occurred.

The news reached London that same morning by telegram:

From principal lighthouse-keeper Ushant: *Drummond Castle* wrecked about midnight June 17 at Ushant. Marquardt sole survivor at Ushant. Two others saved are at Ile Molène. Six bodies recovered, including one officer of the ship about 25 years of age with small light moustache and young girl about six years old. Bodies placed in special house. Kindly telegraph instructions for burial. Ship sank in three minutes.

At about five o'clock in the afternoon the owners, Donald Currie and Company, of Fenchurch Street, received a further telegram:

June 17, 4.10 P.M. *Drummond Castle* total loss off Ushant. Am probably sole survivor. Proceeding London as soon as possible. Marquardt.

How the dreadful thing happened has never been fully explained. The *Drummond Castle* was a ship of 3663 tons, built in Glasgow in 1881. She was on a voyage from South Africa to London. The weather at ten or eleven P.M. on June

16 was similar to that reported the next day, a strong south-
westerly wind and a considerable sea. Visibility was evidently
very poor, so that the look-out had not been able to see the
Ushant light. Despite this, it has never been explained how it
came about that the ship was some twelve miles off her course
and among the dangerous rocks and shoals of that treacherous
coast.

The ship struck the Pierres Vertes, a group of rocks which
lie at the southern entrance of the Fromveur Sound. It was
between half-past ten and eleven o'clock, and almost all, if not
all, the passengers were below. The master, Captain W. W.
Pierce, and his third officer, Brown, were on the bridge.

Captain Pierce does not seem to have realized that his ship
was in immediate danger of foundering. He evidently thought
that the bulkheads would hold and that there was sufficient
time to marshal the passengers and crew. No immediate order
was given for the boats to be lowered, and when this was done
it was too late. Within two or three minutes the ship's decks
were awash, and there was not time to lower a single boat from
the davits. There is no doubt that most of the passengers and
a large part of the ship's company were drowned under
hatches before the ship finally sank. They had no time to
reach the deck.

The frightful swiftness of the disaster explains how it
happened that, although the Breton fishing-fleet was at sea
trawling, there was no suspicion that a disaster had taken
place. No other bodies were at first sighted and very little
wreckage. But at about eight in the morning some cases of
cargo were seen. Those who sighted them did not know that
the passenger Marquardt had been picked up about two hours
before. He was unable to give any account of the matter
until about eight o'clock.

There were tragic scenes in Fenchurch Street around the
offices of the shipping company. Telegrams from anxious
and despairing relatives reached Currie and Company one
after another. The directors knew very little more than their
inquirers, except that they had every reason to fear that their
ship, with passengers and crew, was all but a total loss. There
was only one piece of news that day to reduce the magnitude

of the disaster. Two other survivors were reported safe, both seamen, named Wood and Godbold. They owed their lives to the courage and resource of two French brothers, François and Mathieu Marron. By good fortune, in the hazy weather their boat passed within hail of some wreckage to which two men were clinging. They manned their dinghy in the heavy sea and reached them. It was only just in time, for Wood, either now dead or *in extremis*, had let go and was sinking. Godbold, although much exhausted, was brought in, but it was only with extreme difficulty and at great risk that Wood was pulled into the boat.

The Marron brothers worked on the survivors ceaselessly. Using warm blankets and with artificial respiration doggedly persevered in, they brought Wood back to life, when to save him had seemed hopeless.

There was no comfort from any other quarter. Not only were there but three known survivors, there was no news at first of the discovery of further bodies. This produced an impotent despair, because the directors, pressed for a statement, could say nothing. There was nothing to report but the grim fact that the 103 who made up the crew and the 149 who were the passengers were missing, except for the six bodies and the three survivors named.

It was not until June 19 that more news began to arrive. On that day Mr John Currie, the Company's representative at Havre, said :

. . . the Brest authorities, as is already known, have shown most commendable readiness in co-operating with the British Consul at Brest in making every possible effort to search for survivors and in caring for those who have been rescued.

This was made possible because of the things done by the Breton fishermen and their women. When the tragedy occurred the fleet was at sea; in those days communications were not what they are now. Hardly any of them knew that a ship had been wrecked; none what was the extent of the disaster. At Ushant, Ile Molène, and Ploudalmézeau only the women ashore, the older men, and M. le Curé had details of

the wreck of the *Drummond Castle*. On June 19, still wanting men, these sturdy folk, married women and girls, with their
priest, launched the lifeboat to see if they could find survivors
or bodies. Visibility remained poor, and it still blew hard from
the south-west. They had a rough day of it, and perhaps the
more so that the curé was not an experienced helmsman. For
all that, they would not have been without the support of his
cloth.

This courage and endurance, which was all in the day's
work to them, was not quite in vain. They found no survivors,
for there was none; and it does not appear that they traced
any of the dead that day; but at least they sighted and marked
the position of flotsam and jetsam, whether ashore or still
afloat, as a guide for the organized search which followed.

Although begun that day, it was not until the 20th that the
search could start in earnest. The fleet had returned on the
afternoon tide of the 19th, and the news was passed to them
all. They began at once to scour the islands and coast and such
areas as the lifeboat's reconnaissance suggested.

To Breton fishermen, as to all others, the sea is the old
enemy and the greedy monster which swallows boats and men
and cargoes. To win anything from it, living or dead, is the
kind of victory most worth having, the sweetest kind of solace.
In our own times, when power has replaced sail and so reduced
the hazards, perhaps that instinct still survives to some extent,
but not with the strength it had in 1896. This was the drive
which impelled the Bretons to continue day and night on these
errands of mercy, so that at least they would bring in the dead
and thus defeat and despoil the sea which had claimed them.
From such deeply rooted impulses can spring at one extreme
the wrecker's work and at the other great acts of charity. Had
it been even their own families and those nearest to them who
were so suddenly and tragically missing the search could not
have been more intensive by day and night. On the 19th,
before the lifeboat was manned or any more bodies were discovered, the Curé of Ushant sang a solemn Mass of Requiem.
It was attended by the whole population of the island who
were not at sea.

The dead began to come in. There were but one or two late

on the 19th, but more on the following day. First were two women. One wore a silk dress, without marks whereby the body could be identified. There was no other clue except six sovereigns in one of the pockets. The second wore a gold ring engraved inside with the initials E.M.L.

Every inch of the rocky coast of Ushant and Molène and of the mainland was searched. It yielded on the 19th and 20th forty bodies. Seven were discovered on the mainland and were buried at Ploudalmézeau. The remainder were found either at sea or on the coasts of Molène and Ushant. Mlle Couilmandre sheltered them in her house, and the Curé Abbé le Jeune prepared them for burial. There were many difficulties, the greatest being a shortage of coffins.

Somehow, the bodies were decently housed, until the final preparation could be made, and some were taken to the church for the office of the absolution of the dead. Neither priest nor congregation was concerned as to the faith of those they had snatched from the sea. All alike were fortified with the last rites of the Church. The Abbé's words were heard and remembered not only in France :

> These were men like you toiling to earn their daily bread. Their families were anxiously awaiting their return, and they themselves were impatient to meet their loved ones again. Alas, their poor families will never see them more, but this consolation will at least be vouchsafed to them—they will know that those they mourn rest here in peace in French soil under the shadow of the Cross.

This priest deserved, and in heartfelt gratitude received, more than the decoration which Queen Victoria, through her Government and Ambassador, conferred upon him and some 240 of his parishioners. He not only prayed and exhorted others to work—he worked very hard himself. To him is probably due the first precise indication of the time at which the tragedy occurred. Before the official investigation began, the Abbé made himself responsible for all property found upon the bodies, and particularly for those things which might help in their identification. Among these clues were three watches. All of them had stopped between 11.5 and 11.10. Clearly the *Drummond Castle* had gone down a little short of an hour before midnight. The clothing was carefully examined for all marks; jewellery and any papers or correspondence were exactly catalogued. It was the kind of reward that he would have wished for, that he was able to ask his congregation at Mass to remember the souls of Henry Cohen, William Whipp, Percy Ellis, Alice Reed, and Florence M'Gee. These lie buried in the churchyard at Ushant.

The Abbé le Jeune was elated but dreadfully embarrassed to receive in July a letter from the Archbishop of Canterbury. His reply was precisely what might have been expected of such a man : " Je suis autant plus confus, Monseigneur, que je n'ai strictement accompli que les devoirs que m'imposaient l'humanité et la charité chrétienne. . . ."

It was also in the evening of June 19 that Alphonse Bertillon received urgent official instructions to proceed to Brest and Ushant " to photograph the bodies and to make any notes which might help in the identification of the victims." He left for Brest that night with a photographer and the necessary equipment.

It can hardly have been an enlivening journey, nor a more appropriate one for a retreat into one of his gloomy silences. Never of a sanguine temperament, the prospects of any success in this investigation must have seemed negligible. He could photograph and measure, make his report and send it to London; but at best one or two would be recognized from the data he could supply. There would be no comparative material. The victims were not likely to be people with the kind of record to which his anthropometric methods could be applied with much profit. Why did official authority always think that his scientific method of identification was a kind of magical operation whereby bricks could be produced without straw ?

They came first to Ploudalmézeau, sixteen miles west of Brest. Here was not the heaviest work, for only seven bodies had been brought in. They were decently housed in a temporary morgue upon improvised biers with the crucifix and unbleached lights. With the special equipment he had designed for the purpose of photographing the dead, the victims were supported so that they could be photographed in full face and profile. In two cases there were papers and ornaments whereby identity could be confirmed :

> A marine officer. Papers, envelope addressed to M. C. P. Kingsmell, E. M. A., with letter to my dear husband. Silver watch stopped at 11.5. Sum of £13. Photographs attached for checking with records.
> Woman. 4 rings (1) 5 diamonds in form of rose. (2) 1 ruby and small brilliants. (3) amethyst engraved L McL to A McM. (4) Wedding ring engraved A McM to H McL. Photographs attached for checking with records.

There was one among the bodies which must have aroused his technical interest :

> Woman about 30. Height 6 feet. Features strongly marked of masculine type. Nose very arched. Upper lip with scar like a hair-lip extending from base of nose to middle of lip. Abundant chestnut hair. White corsets lettered in blue " Drew's *A la Grecque*."

This problem of identification was solved. The body was that of Nellie Peachey, who lies at Ploudalmézeau with Harold Stevens and Edward Rich.

For the rest there was a master mechanic and ship's officer with two ribbons on his tunic, a diminutive man of 5 feet 1½ inches, with very small hands and feet, a moustached man of 6 feet, carrying a handkerchief marked E.W., and one in a seaman's jacket with gilt buttons, a boy twelve to fourteen years old . . .

They worked unceasingly. There was not much time, for it was necessary to reach Ushant as soon as possible. No burials were to take place until the bodies had been photographed and described. This was a serious problem for the islanders which must be disposed of as soon as possible.

It was here that the heavy work was to begin, because the bodies were being steadily rescued from the sea. There were already some forty. The work was lightened because the dead had been received as honoured guests. In spite of the labour, it was better ordered than at Ploudalmézeau. The Abbé le Jeune must have greatly helped the work with his carefully docketed exhibits. Although perhaps with different motives, he was as interested in the problem of identification as Bertillon.

There were also obstacles stemming from this same reverence for the dead. The people did not like the candles—which all Bretons love so much—being disturbed when the examination was being made, and among the women who watched the dead there was some primordial fear of the photography. It must have reached its highest point when they came to examine the greatest treasure won from the sea. There was a little improvised bier high banked with white roses. Wrapped in spotless linen, a child not more than twelve months old lay on it. Around it were Breton women, in their heavy black gowns and white gauzy head-dresses, lamenting. They began seemingly to protest at the violation of this shrine, but they could not, or would not, speak except in their Celtic dialect, of which Bertillon understood not a single word. There was an interpreter near by.

" They say please not to disturb the candles and the crucifix, and they do not want the child touched or photographed."

" We will not disturb the candles, but tell them we have a duty to do just as they have. This may help the little one's family."

They made way for them at that, even if still with some fear of the neatly dressed, saturnine figure with his mysterious and sinister apparatus. The fear must have gone when they saw the extreme gentleness with which Bertillon raised the child's head and body to adjust the supports for the photography in routine full face and profile. It was most doubtful if the photographs would assist in the identification, but, because the possibility of ultimate recognition existed, the record must be made.

They went in to continue the work while the women closed round the small catafalque, taking up their dirge invoking Madame Marie of Good Succour and their strange Breton saints.

It was an exhausting adventure, lasting two or three days. That no detailed records of Bertillon's work remain is unfortunate, for it leaves a gap not only in his personal history, but in that of the science of identification itself. On June 27 the directors of Donald Currie and Company reported that fifty-three bodies (a high percentage in the circumstances) had been recovered. They had received twenty-seven "official descriptions," by which presumably was meant those founded upon Bertillon's reports and photographs. Of these, ten bodies had been positively identified. It is probable that, in fact, further identifications were confirmed later. With one exception we do not know what were the complete results of an experiment which is unique in the history of identification. There is, however, little doubt that Bertillon's photographs and description of the tall lady with the masculine features proved her identity, and that much of the other evidence he assembled was essential in identifying the remaining bodies.

He was decorated on June 17, 1897, the anniversary of the disaster, with the *Drummond Castle* Medal by the British Ambassador. There are no details of the ceremony, but the presentation was on a separate occasion, unconnected with the public awards at Ushant and Brest, when large numbers of medals were bestowed. It was evidently recognized that his services were of a special character and value, and therefore to be marked by an independent official gesture. He treasured the medal even above more intrinsically valuable distinctions, but he never spoke of the occasion of its presentation. Among his other phobias Bertillon had a horror of all official functions, and he listened always with exasperated embarrassment to the clichés and platitudes (as he thought them) of the official speech of welcome, honourable mention, or the like.

Whether he was satisfied with the results of the hard and conscientious labours in which the disaster of the *Drummond Castle* involved him we do not know. Probably he was not. But Great Britain, the country he most admired and respected after his own, had signified her feelings in the matter. At least he had a just cause for satisfaction in that.

18. THE COMPETITIVE SYSTEM

AT the same period, and perhaps in the same year that Bertillon won his battle for anthropometry, the kind of reverse he had met with in 1879 was being re-enacted at Scotland Yard. The casualty was in this case a Scottish physician, named Faulds. In his book *Guide to Fingerprint Identification*, published in 1905, he says that between 1886 and 1888 he had personal interviews with officials at Scotland Yard and in particular with Inspector J. B. Tunbridge regarding the use of fingerprints as a means of identification. He had expressed himself willing to set up a small bureau free of charge to test the value of his method.

M. Andrieux had considered Bertillon insane. Scotland Yard thought Faulds was a crank. "How could anyone be convicted," some one said, "on identification of features confined within so small a space as the tip or pad of a finger?"

Inspector Tunbridge was more far-seeing than most of his colleagues. Although the document has not survived, it appears that he made a report in 1887 which was not entirely unfavourable. He thought the system was accurate, but could not see how it could be applied in practice. Tunbridge was to change his mind later. When he became Commissioner of Police in New Zealand he was largely responsible for the introduction of the system there.

It would require a separate volume to pursue the dismal history of the fingerprint controversy, and it would be beyond our scope. But Faulds is well within it, both as a human being and a research worker in the field of identification. There are many respects in which the characters of Faulds and Bertillon can be compared. Both had virtues markedly Roman in quality, and they shared a temperament at once aloof and ferocious which made co-operation with others extremely difficult. If they ever corresponded the writings have not been preserved, and it is perhaps fortunate that they never met. They would certainly have quarrelled. The result of this would have been that Bertillon would have become embroiled in the controversies of Galton, Herschel, and Faulds, and would have thus contributed a further irritant to a situation already sufficiently confused by personal animosities.

As it was, Bertillon remained outside the fingerprint controversy. This was greatly to his own advantage, and still more so to that of the progress of research into the problems of identification. He specifically disclaimed any part in the formulation of the theory or practice of fingerprint identification, so that it seems at first sight all the more singular that in many respects he should have done in the early stages more than the original claimants to advance it.

Although there is now no trace of the correspondence, Faulds claimed to have written to the Chief of the Paris Police in 1880 drawing attention to his discovery of fingerprints as a means of identification. There is no reason to doubt his claim, for he had written to many well-known scientific men throughout the world, including Charles Darwin. Faulds was at this time in Japan as a medical missionary, and the work he did there should of itself ensure him a place in social history. But his epoch-making work was that which he described in a letter written from his Tokyo hospital and published in *Nature* on October 28, 1880. He told his readers what he had learnt about fingerprints; he described the patterns; he knew that certain apes had prints very similar to those of human beings; his method of taking finger impressions was precisely the same as that used to-day; most vital of all, he knew that there were many surfaces upon which the fingers could leave an exact reproduction of their pattern, so that the individual, if his prints had been recorded, could be identified *in absentia*. No one can deprive Faulds of the high distinction of having made this last discovery, perhaps the most significant in all the history of identification.

This is not the place to pursue that. What is now to our purpose is that if Faulds' communication was sent to the Chief of the Paris Police in 1880 it must ultimately have reached

Andrieux's hands at the very time that he was wrestling with the problem of the eccentric behaviour of his most junior Prefecture clerk. It is unfortunate but not surprising that Faulds' letter has not survived. Probably it got no further than the wastepaper basket of an already much tried official.

There is no direct evidence that Bertillon was aware of Faulds' work. This is explicable in the light of the fact that he wrote very little, and that he shared a defect of character very common then. It was a failure to acknowledge the work of others in the same or in related fields. Even Galton not only minimized the contributions which Faulds had made to fingerprint science, but tried to discredit them altogether. Herschel was more generous, but never gave Faulds his due. There was some reason for this, since Faulds, with a disproportionate sense of grievance, grossly overstated his case and used to pillory men with whom he should at least have tried to co-operate. It is an unfortunate reflection upon the destructively competitive elements too often traceable even in the scientific attitude of that time.

Indirectly there is strong evidence that Bertillon must have known of Faulds' work, although it may not have been before 1888. The name of one of the men who made fingerprint history is very little known in England. It is Forgeot. In 1891 his thesis *Les Empreintes Digitales étudiées au point de vue Médico-judiciaire*, sponsored by Lacassagne's laboratory at Lyon, was published. Forgeot was acquainted with the work of Faulds, and he recognized the vital importance of fingerprint traces as a means of identifying the individual *in absentia*. He was among the first to devise methods of developing fingerprints—that is to say, of treating them with powders or chemicals to make them fully visible. His classic work has never been fully recognized. However this may be, Lacassagne was Bertillon's life-long friend. Both knew Forgeot, and so, by inescapable inference, of the work of Faulds.

Bertillon has been credited with the creation of the fingerprint system. On the other hand, it has been suggested that he disliked it and did everything he could to discourage its development. Both these verdicts are wrong, and are, I think, founded upon a misunderstanding of the Bertillon psychology.

He was extremely cautious on account of his commendably scientific attitude of mind; but this caution was exaggerated by reason of the defects of his theoretical equipment. He did not, as shall be seen in another connexion, really understand the principles of the calculus of probability. Had he done so he would have recognized that his anthropometric system alone was sufficient to identify the person. The elaboration of the *portrait parlé*, to which we owe so much, had its source, oddly enough, in Bertillon's uncertain grasp of some elementary mathematical principles.

It is thus not surprising to hear him echoing those at Scotland Yard who had said, " How could anyone be convicted on identification of features confined within so small a space as the top or pad of a finger? " Those are the words he used, or words to that effect.

This is well known. What is less well known is that he could have appealed to the authority of Faulds in support of it. In a more than usually disagreeable letter to *Nature* in 1917 (three years after the death of Bertillon) this is what Faulds wrote :

> A most curious confusion has arisen from an original police blunder that no two single finger patterns are ever alike, for which, I think, Sir William [Herschel] himself is mainly responsible. I am sure there is no scientific basis for such an assertion.

It might have been Bertillon himself speaking. Faulds must have read Galton's book on fingerprints, written twenty-five years before. In it the great statistician had said that the chances against two finger patterns being alike was 64,000,000,000 to 1. The truth must be that Faulds, like Bertillon, was unable to appreciate the formal mathematical proofs of identity.

This lingering suspicion, with him to his life's end, was the root cause of Bertillon's dislike of fingerprints.

But if he disliked fingerprints they fascinated that inquiring mind. With very sound judgment he placed fingerprints in the same category as his " special marks " which may have little identification value individually, but, taken together with others, can show an unique relation. This led directly to a piece of research which for some time remained unique in fingerprint history. These are what he called " the professional signs."

In 1892 he published at the request of Lozé, then Prefect of Police, a list of the special marks found upon fingerprints together with a remarkable series of photographs. They represented changes on the skin surfaces produced by repetitive operations. Seamstresses showed punctured prints on the left hand if they were right-handed, and vice versa. Florists had punctures upon all the fingers. They were due in both cases to the continued pricks of needle or thorn. Continued contact with alkaline water wore down the ridge-marking on the fingers of laundresses. Parchment-like callouses were found on the fingers of the left hand of glass-workers. The surface took the ink badly so that good impressions could not be had. This work inspired others in South America, Italy, and Belgium, where thousands of ' professional ' prints were examined to decide if these peculiarities and others noted by Bertillon were sufficiently specific to be identifiable.

If Bertillon had doubts, common enough at that time, concerning the uniqueness of the fingerprint pattern he at once grasped its great significance in criminal investigation. What he said of fingerprints in general was typical of that hard-headed common sense which was one of his notable characteristics. Anthropometry could do all that fingerprints could do in the field of identification, and more. Its shortcoming was that the lawbreaker did not leave his anthropometric measurements behind him on the scene of the crime.

As has been seen, Bertillon was responsible for the first case in France wherein fingerprint evidence was used to convict a murderer, but the success did not convince him that fingerprints alone could identify the individual with absolute certainty.

This doubt remained until his life's end. In 1912, two years before his death, he published an article in the *Archives of Lacassagne* which purported to show that the points of resemblance upon two fingerprints of different origin might in certain circumstances show an apparent correspondence. The article was illustrated with the excellent photographs he knew so well how to take. They were ingeniously reproduced, to indicate how, if certain portions of the pattern were not shown, what remained might suggest correspondences which would produce an appearance of identity in different finger-prints. This thesis was purely academic. It did not explain how the artificial conditions he created to produce these frag-mentary designs could have occurred in practice. Advocates of the fingerprint system, which was now well established, also declared that his ' points of resemblance ' were not points of resemblance at all, since they showed only the same general form.

These doubts never checked his research, which he pursued with the dogged patience characteristic of all that he did. He was by no means the first to investigate methods of developing fingerprints, but he was in the vanguard. Having little know-ledge of chemistry, he was not well acquainted with the physical and chemical properties of materials. He used a methodical empiricism. Bertillon experimented with practi-cally every known solid which could be reduced to a fine powder to discover which kinds of particle would adhere most intimately to the greasy ridge-marks of the finger pattern and produce the best contrast. This reminds us that we owe the discovery that the oxides of the heavy metals are in general the most efficient developing powders to him, and the finely powdered red lead still used by the French police to develop fingerprints. When a fingerprint was found on a dark surface he experimented with white powders.

The evidence that Bertillon utilized fingerprints at an early stage is thus overwhelming. In Europe 1902 is a milestone in fingerprint history. Bertillon was not long anticipated by Scot-land Yard. The first recorded case of fingerprint evidence of identification appears to be that of Harry Jackson, who was tried at the Central Criminal Court for burglary on September 13, 1902, the crime having taken place in the previous June. We shall recall that the murder of Reibel took place on October 17 of the same year.

It was not the use of fingerprints but their function as a

primary means of describing and identifying individuals which Bertillon disliked. At the time that he was advancing the uses of fingerprints he was also defending his own system in his candid fashion :

> My system has now been in use for twenty years. We have accumulated millions of cards. If fingerprints were to be used to the full tens of millions would be necessary because it cannot have its full value unless a ' single fingerprint ' system is used. This would require ten extra cards for each person. . . . It is not a question of my own system being replaced little by little by the new classification, supposing, of course, that the Administration would give me the necessary accommodation and personnel. It would be labour lost if the new classification were not founded upon a clear, precise, and rational ' single fingerprint ' classification. All my colleagues' classifications depend upon a system wherein *ten prints appear on the same card*. It is very much less instructive for the police who have in their possession under this system only two or three fingerprints which are not fully descriptive of the suspected person.

There is a good deal of force in this; but, most significantly, it exposes Bertillon's lingering doubts concerning the complete efficacy of identification by fingerprints. He evidently thought that something much more detailed and elaborate was necessary to ensure absolutely conclusive results.

But there was another and a less worthy reason for Bertillon's lack of enthusiasm for fingerprint classification in general. The quoted passage implies, and it was indeed the fact, that Bertillon never properly understood the fingerprint classification he so briefly dismisses. A personal rather than an intellectual reaction was responsible for this. As shall now be seen, Bertillon harboured deeply rooted feelings of animosity against a man to whom belongs the merit of having devised the first rational and workable system of the classification of fingerprints; and to this day no one knows precisely why.

19. BERTILLON AND VUCETICH

THERE are a number of accounts of this unfortunate incident, and none of them is much to Alphonse Bertillon's credit. He was at no time very popular with journalists, and one of them once circulated an account of the affair which owed a good deal to a vivid and malicious imagination. The report was that when Juan Vucetich came to call upon Bertillon during his world tour in 1913 the great man not only grossly insulted his visitor from the Argentine, but made a physical assault upon him into the bargain. Having regard to the state of Bertillon's health in 1913, this seems improbable. For more than twelve months before his death in 1914 he was a very sick man and incapable of physical violence, even if he had been tempted to use it. But that he treated Vucetich with a brutality and rudeness which deeply wounded him there is no doubt.

The card which Juan Vucetich presented when he called at the Department of Judicial Identity has been preserved. As the creator of the first complete system of classification of fingerprints, Vucetich evidently thought he was entitled to call upon Bertillon without giving notice of his intended visit. The Chief of the Service clearly thought otherwise. To call upon Bertillon without an appointment was to risk a severe snub, if nothing worse, and in the later years he became even less accessible than he had been formerly. There was a time when, if in the mood, he would receive unannounced visitors, even the journalists he so much feared and hated; but this occasion was unfortunately not one of them. The account of the matter given by Bertillon's niece, Mlle Suzanne Bertillon, is perhaps the only one upon which it would be safe to rely.

Vucetich arrived one morning, evidently expecting to be received immediately and with open arms. He had to wait in an outer office which was a kind of guard-room of the Holy of Holies, and it has been said that he had to wait a very long time. Suddenly the door leading to Bertillon's office was flung wide open. The Chief of the Service stood on the threshold. He treated his visitor to a hostile scrutiny which slowly passed from head to feet.

" Sir," he said, " you have tried to do me a great deal of harm." [Vous avez essayé de me faire beaucoup de mal, monsieur.]

He slammed the door in the face of Vucetich. It was the first and last occasion upon which they met.

Inexcusable in any event, it was the more so because this visitor was no lackey or self-seeker, but a man of Bertillon's own calibre, who may well have come, not only for an exchange of ideas, but to acknowledge his debt to the creator of the first system of identification. It is much to the credit of Vucetich that he hardly ever spoke of the matter. When he did so it was to say that they had met once only and had agreed in nothing except that each should go his own way. [. . . desde entonces cada cual siguió por el camino de su propria suerte.]

Interpreted against the background of Bertillon's life and work, Vucetich's career may answer the riddle of the great man's violence and animosity. It is possible that he really believed that Vucetich had tried to injure his reputation. The man he treated so roughly was certainly innocent of any deliberate attempt to minimize the value of his discovery. What he had done was to use something else which was to prove a more efficient substitute for the Bertillon system. He can hardly with fairness be blamed for that. Nevertheless, it is an irony of history that Vucetich's discovery was to ruin his own reputation and to destroy the honour he ought to have had as a prophet in his own country.

To Vucetich belongs the high distinction of having devised the first practical system of fingerprint classification. Born in Dalmatia in 1858, he emigrated to the Argentine in 1884. Like Bertillon, he had no academic education, and it appears that he joined the Argentine police when he arrived in the country. He must have received rapid promotion, since in 1889 he was appointed chief of the Anthropometric Bureau of Identification, attached to the Provincial Police of Buenos Aires, with headquarters at La Plata. The adoption of the Bertillon system had been recommended by Dr Drago, who had visited France to study anthropometry, and it was the Bertillon system which Vucetich first organized from La Plata. In 1891 his attention was drawn to a French report of Galton's lecture *Patterns in Thumb and Finger Marks*. By September 1891 he had already devised a system of classification based on the patterns of the ten fingers. It is true that he owed a certain amount to Galton's classification, but he went much further in devising a workable system, which Galton did not. It was in operation in September 1891. A few of the original record-cards bearing that date are still in existence.

His enthusiasm for the new system was due in part to the fact that he never liked the anthropometric system and made no secret of the fact although he was officially obliged to retain it. This is what he said at the Conference on fingerprints at La Plata in 1901:

> I can assure you that from 1891 until 1895, the years during which we used the anthropometric system, never, in spite of all our efforts, were we able to determine with certainty the identity of an individual by means of measurement because we always found differences for the same person. For this reason we adopted fingerprints.

It is not difficult to imagine the indignation with which the illustrious creator of anthropometry greeted these blasphemous words when they came to his ears. And it is probable that they did so almost immediately. Vucetich's fingerprint system was very far from being universally popular. Indeed, there grew up in the Argentine a Bertillon and an anti-Bertillon party, just as there were in France Dreyfusards and anti-Dreyfusards. Bertillon advocates probably lost no time in publicizing as widely as possible what Vucetich had said, with suitable comment. This criticism was certainly unjust to the anthropometric system. Under suitable conditions, it is quite practicable to identify the individual by means of measurement. Vucetich's experience in the Argentine was due to his lack of well-trained personnel. The system was much more difficult to operate than that of fingerprints, whose records could be compiled by the comparatively simple process of placing printing-ink upon the finger and pressing that finger upon a piece of paper.

In spite of the violent opposition to them in certain quarters, fingerprints had a spectacular success. Opponents of the new method must have been severely shaken by the Rojas case of 1892. A woman named Francesca Rojas, of Necochea, in the Province of Buenos Aires, accused a neighbour of murdering her two sons. He was arrested. It was later clearly proved that the bloody fingermarks found on the scene of the crime corresponded to those of the woman. She was convicted of the crime on this evidence alone. The official records of this case have unfortunately been lost; but it establishes beyond doubt that Vucetich was the first expert to secure a conviction upon fingerprints as the sole clue.

But his great achievement was not that he ran to earth a murderer or thief here and there by the discovery of fingerprints on the scene of the crime. Even to-day it is not generally understood that the chief problem of fingerprints or any other system of identification is the problem of search. If there is a collection of, say, five hundred fingerprints the required record can be found without much trouble, whatever the system of arrangement. But because the number of prints increased day by day, a system had to be devised which could deal, not with hundreds, but with millions of cases. It is undeniable that Vucetich devised the first system by dividing his fingerprints into four main types which he called arches, internal loops, external loops, and whorls. These designs when found on the thumb were described by letters of the alphabet, and when on the fingers by numbers. These are examples of the formulæ:

$$A \ 1244 \qquad E \ 3221$$

In the first the thumb has an arch and the fingers an arch, an internal loop, a whorl, and a whorl in that order; in the second, the thumb has an external loop, the fingers an external loop, an internal loop, an internal loop, and an arch in that order.

It is possible to combine these four designs on the five fingers in 4^5—that is to say, 1024—different ways, and the same designs in the two hands in 4^{10}, or 1,048,576, different ways. These theoretically possible combinations were provided for in a filing cabinet containing 180 drawers. Since the possible combinations are known, and the number of divisions determined, it is clear that the position in the cabinet of any set of prints is predetermined.

This principle of providing for every possible combination of primary fingerprint patterns within a given number of drawers and files is fundamental to every fingerprint system. Henry, for example, the creator of the famous English system, ingeniously combined the fingers of both hands in one formula so that the possible combinations of the primary classification of both hands is reduced to 4^5, or 1024. But, although elaborated and improved, the principle of his system, introduced in 1896, is the same. He further elaborated his cabinet by dividing it into 1024 (32^2) divisions, so that each primary classified set of prints had a division to itself.

Thus came into existence his classic formula:

$$\frac{L \quad L \quad W \quad W}{L \quad W \quad L \quad W}$$

which represents every combination of a pair of fingerprints consisting of either a loop or a whorl. For the two hands, five pairs, the possible combinations are 4^5, or 1024. In the matter of their arrangement in the cabinet, Henry said this in the first edition of his book, published in 1900: " The number 1024 is the square of 32, so a cabinet containing 32 sets of 32 pigeonholes arranged horizontally would provide locations for all combinations of Loops and Whorls of the two digits taken in pairs." Henry was able to utilize the formula by using a device which had not occurred to Vucetich. He began, in fact, with four types of design—arches, loops, whorls, and composites. To devise his formula, he ' approximated ' arches to loops and composites to whorls. This is practical, because the number of loops and whorls is very large in comparison with the number of arches and composites. In the primary classification it was therefore unnecessary to treat them separately. The devising of a formula the individual elements of which could be accommodated within 1024 divisions is one of the most significant discoveries in the history of fingerprint classification.

Nevertheless, the Vucetich system, less consistently elaborated though it is than Henry's, is still in use in the Argentine and in the larger South American states. It is more popular now than it was in the lifetime of its creator, whose very enthusiasm for the system he had introduced produced political repercussions of a very violent character. Vucetich, largely because the problem of personal identification was the ruling passion of his life, had persistently advocated the fingerprinting of the entire Argentine population. No attempt was made to act upon this until 1916, when, to his immense satisfaction, the Government proposed to set up a General Register of Identification. This envisaged the recording of the fingerprints of all Argentine subjects, and of all foreigners resident in the country. The Bill was passed by vote on July 18 and became law on July 20. On August 3, 1916, Vucetich was appointed Director of the Register.

It appears that from the first there was considerable opposition. With strong views on the liberty of the subject, substantial sections of the population refused to obey the law. There were arrests. These stern measures, far from improving the situation, produced serious riots. Vucetich himself was extremely unpopular, and there were grave incidents in which the General Register itself was attacked and its windows broken.

By the following May the situation had become so serious that the Government ordered the repeal of the law regarding the General Register. Not only this: there was a direction to destroy all the identification records which had been compiled. They were burnt by order of Don José Luis Cautilo on May 28, 1917. Vucetich never recovered from this blow which destroyed what he believed to be the most important development of his life's work. He immediately went into retirement in the small town of Dolores, where he died in 1926.

Bertillon died twelve years earlier, leaving no complete clue as to the reasons for his intense animosity towards a man whose achievements matched his own. It has been said that he was of the opinion that Vucetich had borrowed from his system of

anthropometric classification and utilized it without acknowledgment in connexion with fingerprints. If he ever made this
accusation it was monstrously unjust and manifestly absurd.

It seems more probable that a mixture of personal and professional sentiments was at the root of Bertillon's enmity.
There is no doubt that the most successful practitioners of
anthropometry were those who had been trained by Bertillon
personally. He regarded Vucetich, who had then never been
to Paris, as an amateur who in condemning the system was,
in fact, condemning his own incompetence.

The personal sentiments can perhaps be deduced from a
study of Vucetich's photograph. It depicts a man the exact
opposite to Bertillon. Here is a robust physique, great physical
energy, and marked self-assurance. These were all the qualities
which Bertillon lacked, and, in particular, the self-assurance.
Even if their technical and professional disagreements rankled
with him it is likely enough that Vucetich's rather ornate
visiting-card with no message upon it requesting an appointment, as if such a matter ought to be taken for granted, was
the precipitating cause of Bertillon's violent and apparently
unreasonable hostility.

20. BERTILLON AND HENRY

BERTILLON'S almost baseless quarrel with Vucetich cannot, as already suggested, be explained by reference to his dislike of any criticism of his system. There was a more personal cause for the unpleasantness at the Prefecture when Vucetich called there. Sir Edward Henry also became as definite a critic of Bertillonage as Vucetich. But his criticism was founded upon a more detailed study and a much greater experience of the system than Vucetich could claim. His acknowledgment also of Bertillon's work as a pioneer was better informed and more generous.

The system [of Bertillon] was first practically worked in France in 1890, and soon began to yield such gratifying results that it has since, in a more or less modified form, gradually been adopted by most countries. It represents a scientific solution of what had long been claimed an insoluble problem, and is obviously an enormous improvement upon all rough-and-ready means previously adopted, one of the best-known and most successful of which was that of indexing persons according to tattoo marks. Many of the criminal classes are addicted to the practice of having their arms and bodies tattooed, and this fact was turned to account by the police authorities, who started a tattoo index, which, on the whole, has rendered them much useful help.

This was a very different approach to the matter if it is compared with the hasty judgment of Vucetich when he said that two series of measurements were never found to agree if made at different times on the same individual. Like Bertillon, Vucetich does not seem to have had a systematized technical education, and, less conscious of his limitations, he was less cautious. Henry, on the other hand, was a better mathematician than Bertillon. He also had a better theoretical equipment to deal with the problems of classification, and particularly those of fingerprints.

He introduced the anthropometric system into the Province of Bengal in 1892. It was gradually extended to many other provinces in India. In 1898 some 200,000 records had been produced.

Henry's experience of the system was wider than that of Vucetich, and his judgment of it was therefore much better informed. He really knew what were the advantages and disadvantages of the method.

That the eleven bodily measurements could readily be made by almost anyone after a short period of training was an article in the Bertillon creed. This was not borne out by Henry. " Measurers," he said, " must be put through a special course of instruction and be possessed of sufficient education to understand the significance of the figures on the decimal scale." Perhaps the main reason for the difference of their experience was that in France the decimal system was in universal use, and therefore part of all elementary education. In India, where the general standard of instruction was poor and where the English system of measurement was taught, the trainee was required to learn a system which was fundamentally unfamiliar.

This influenced the whole operation of filing. Every one with experience of office routine knows what difficulties and delays can result from the misfiling of correspondence. The misfiling of an identity-card because the data recorded upon it are incorrect may make it almost impossible to trace the card at all. There are two possibilities of error. If the measurements are incorrect by even a small amount, either because they are wrongly made or wrongly read off, the card will be misplaced in the file, and it will be impossible to match it or to correct the mistake at a later stage without an intensive search. Even this may not be successful.

The error need not be large. An inaccuracy of measurement or recording may result in a card being placed in some section very far removed from its proper position.

To overcome this difficulty, in India each measurement was made three times and an average taken. In practice the number of measurements had to be reduced from eleven to six, because it would have been impracticable to make thirty-three measurements of each individual.

Despite this restricted use, the figures show how vastly superior anthropometry was to the rule-of-thumb methods used before. In 1893 there were 23 identifications; in 1894, 143, in 1895, 207, and in 1896, 334. The sharp drop in the figures for 1897, 1898, and 1899 (318, 148, and 59) was, of course, due to the progressive substitution of fingerprints for bodily measurements. Over the same period there was a very steep rise in the number of cases of identification by finger-prints (from 345 in 1898 to 569 in 1899). This also suggested that identification by fingerprints was not only a simpler but a more efficient method of identifying the individual.

As has been seen, this was contrary to Bertillon's opinion. His conviction was that proof did not exist that fingerprint patterns were individually unique. The statistical proof of the much-admired Galton had not been sufficient to convince him of this.

Bertillon certainly never accepted the view that as a means of identification fingerprints were superior to anthropometry. He never, in fact, claimed infallibility for his own system, although all the experimental evidence went to show that it was completely reliable. During his thirty years of office at the Department of Judicial Identity it does not appear that a single case of confusion of identity occurred. He naturally had a more intimate knowledge of the technique and a greater experience of it in practice than any other authority, and his opinion in this respect must be accepted as final.

In this connexion it is interesting to refer back to the facts and figures of the Will West case, which is so often quoted as the rock upon which the Bertillon system broke. It is not so in fact. The recorded measurements of these two Negroes were as follow :

Will West No. 3246
19.7; 15.8; 12.3; 28.2; 50.2; 1.78.5; 9.7; 91.3; 1.87.0; 6.6; 14.8.

Will West No. 2626
19.8; 15.9; 12.2; 27.5; 50.3; 1.77.5; 9.6; 91.3; 1.88.0; 6.6; 14.8.

These measurements were said to be " identical for practical purposes " by those reporting upon them. Bertillon's comment upon this case is not on record, but there can be no doubt as to what his comment would have been. The figures certainly show a remarkably close correspondence, but the fourth set (the foot measurement) reveals a variation of seven millimetres. This was a divergence far beyond the limit of allowed operational error. If one of Bertillon's assistants had made a mistake of seven millimetres in a total length of twenty-eight centimetres he would have been in considerable trouble with the chief of his department. These figures would not have been accepted by Bertillon as " identical for practical purposes."

For this reason he was opposed to any modification of his system. Even the eleven measurements were not regarded as sufficient and final proof of identity. They were supplemented with the colour of the eyes, the hair, and the pigmentation of the skin, so that in all at least fourteen points of resemblance were regarded as necessary for formal proof.

It is one of the disadvantages of the Bertillon system that it is less easy to apply internationally than the fingerprint method. India, where his distinguished British contemporary was first called upon to deal with the problem of identification, would have been Bertillon's despair. He would have been obliged, as Henry was, to reduce and simplify the measurement technique. Inaccuracies and mistakes would have been a continual exasperation. He would have had to abandon the supplementary descriptions of eye, hair, and skin colour which were so important a part of his method, for the coloured races do not show sufficient variations in pigmentation to make their description of any value. Even had he wished to do so he could not have fairly criticized the truncated application of anthropometry in India. It had to be used in this restricted form if it were to be used at all.

India was the country wherein the system of identification now universally accepted originated. Bertillon was the first in the field only because he immediately recognized the implications of his discovery. The great man used to complain, with justice, of the unreasonable obstacles he had to overcome before the significance of his discovery was recognized. He did not then know that Sir William Herschel had discovered fingerprints, although he had not pursued the matter, when Bertillon was still a ' problem child ' of five years old. But, on account of the fact that Herschel's discovery suffered the same fate in India as had Bertillon's in France, it was *Bertillonage* which was first officially adopted in India, even if not in a form which its illustrious promoter could approve.

It was also used in some form by Scotland Yard. In July 1900 a committee known as the Belper Committee was sitting to study the merits of measurement and fingerprints as methods of identification. It was then that Sir Edward Henry was asked the historic question by the Chairman, Lord Belper :

" Is this system [of classifying fingerprints] an invention of your own ? "

" Yes."

As is well known, the result was the introduction of Henry's system of fingerprints as the sole identification technique in England in the following year.

Fingerprints had, however, been in use in England before, together with a system of measurement. This was by reason of the pioneer work of Henry, Galton, Faulds, and Herschel. The reason it had not developed was not on account of a failure to appreciate the merits of the system as a means of identification. The unsolved problem was a practical system of classification so that the required identification record could be found among many hundreds of thousands and compared with the new record when the individual appeared again.

It is in this connexion that Henry and Bertillon stand together as the pioneers of the system of the identification of the individual as an applied science and as the promoters of one of the most important discoveries of the nineteenth century.

No one could fairly say of the distinguished man who devised our English system of fingerprint classification that he was slow to acknowledge his debt to other workers in his chosen field. He certainly paid a generous, if deserved, tribute to Bertillon in acknowledging the merits of the anthropometric primary classification. It appears in the first edition of his classic book, *The Classification and Uses of Fingerprints*:

> The strongest feature of anthropometry is the excellence of the system of primary classification whereby the cards are distributed according to the length and breadth of the head, length of left middle finger, length of left fore arm, and length of left foot, amongst 243 pigeon-holes. By an arrangement somewhat similar in principle, upon determination whether the pattern on each digit taken in turn is a Whorl or not a Whorl, finger impressions are, in primary classification, rapidly distributed amongst 1024 pigeon-holes, and effective means of splitting up accumulations by secondary classification are provided. [See Appendix II.]

Bertillon often failed to recognize his debt to others, but it would not be fair to him to suggest that in the matter of the classification of identifiable characteristics he owed anything to the creators of fingerprint classification. It is undeniable that he was the first to formulate a system and to lay down its principles. All his successors owe something to this fundamental work. Curiously enough, the system of fingerprint arrangement he adopted when fingerprints were added to his anthropometric records was based upon a classification which resembles that of Vucetich; but he indignantly repudiated the suggestion that he owed anything to the Argentine system. If he borrowed anything from it he had no appreciation of its best features. His own method of classification was far from satisfactory, and was perhaps an index of his lack of confidence in the fingerprint as an ultimate means of identification. The truth is that Bertillon, having no interest in fingerprints as a means of identification of criminals after arrest, was not concerned with a system of classification primarily intended for that purpose. When an accused or suspected person was brought to him he turned not to the finger impression but to the anthropometric description upon which his classification was always based. His real motive for adding the record of fingerprints to his anthropometric cards was his conviction of the value of fingerprints as clues of identity left behind on the scene of the crime. If he did not accept their unique value as marks of identity he never had any doubt as to their great significance as *corpus delicti*. It was for this reason that he stressed the value of a single-fingerprint classification.

He never, however, made an attempt to devise a system of single-fingerprint classification of his own. The fingerprints always remained an integral part of the anthropometric classification. This considerably complicated his problem of search when it was required to match impressions found on the scene of a crime with those in his collection.

If he did not accept Galton's proof of the uniqueness of fingerprints he had a high opinion of the Henry classification, which he would no doubt have used himself if he had substituted fingerprints for anthropometry. As shall be seen, when Henry's second-in-command paid a visit to Bertillon's department judicial photography rather than fingerprints or anthropometry may have proved their chief interest in common. It is certain that the welcome given to the official from Scotland Yard was very different to that which Vucetich received.

21. HORA TENEBRARUM

BERTILLON'S association with the Dreyfus tragedy is a problem which on the face of it looks insoluble. Perhaps the reason for this is to be found, or at least sought, not only in the psychology of the man himself, complex and contradictory as it was, but in the history and social situation of the period. Of scientific men it has been said with a good deal of truth that they do not necessarily apply the rigidly objective methods which their profession imposes upon them in matters outside their vocational field, and that in matters of religion economics, or politics they are as fallible as, or more so than any ordinary man in the street.

The fact that there is some truth in this does not make i less unsafe as a generalization, but it can be applied with a good deal of force to the situation created by the Dreyfu disturbance. The documents of the period, from the news papers to the partisan pamphlets, make depressing reading, fo they show how the whole French nation, from scientist to road sweeper, was split into two violently hostile camps because of a piece of translucent paper called the *bordereau* which no more than a score of people had ever seen.

Perhaps for this reason, and for others which shall appear the whole truth concerning this ambiguous document was no and now never can be discovered. So far as is known, the *bordereau* no longer exists. There is no original photograph of it, although some reproductions appeared in the newspapers a the time, notably in *Le Matin* of December 10, 1896. It wa not appreciated at the time, even by some of the experts who examined it, that this reproduction, said to be the best, was no from a photograph but was an engraving. It was made by Teysonières, who professed competence in the identification of handwriting because he was an engraver. In view of

Teysonières' subsequent career we are entitled to feel a little doubtful concerning what he might have done in copying a document which he declared was in the handwriting of Dreyfus. Although it was not in connexion with this notorious matter, Teysonières was convicted of perjury in 1901.

The fact that he was later proved a dishonest man does not show that he consciously attempted to approximate his engraving to the handwriting of Dreyfus. So far as we know there is no evidence of that. What he did was to find, in his superficial and incompetent *expertise*, what he was expected to find.

This dubious relic looks almost respectable among a host of quite outrageous contemporaries. The most sensational of them was an alleged photograph of a copy of the original document with copious notes said to have been written with the German Emperor's own hand.

In any kind of criminal inquiry circumstantial evidence, when interpreted by technical methods, is claimed as being of great value, because it is a substitute for the fallible evidence of eye-witnesses. If ever sound circumstantial evidence were needed it was needed in this affair. The best minds and the most charitable hearts were filled by an up-surge of passion and prejudice which made an objective judgment almost impossible for anyone. You were a Dreyfusard or an anti-Dreyfusard, and there could be nothing in between. Small wonder that the matter should have nearly brought about successfully a *coup d'état* by a convinced Dreyfus advocate and that a highly placed Frenchman, an anti-Dreyfusard, should have violently assaulted President Loubet, revisionist successor to the anti-Dreyfusard Faure, and nearly killed him. Such an atmosphere makes it impossible to interpret the written or spoken evidence. It makes even the confessions of the principal villains in the piece ambiguous in themselves.

If the notorious *bordereau* is still, after all, in existence in some archive, and if it ever comes to light, it would be a find almost as priceless as the discovery of a Shakespeare manuscript. With the original document and suitable standard writings, it might be possible to rewrite certain pages of the scandalous history of the Dreyfus Affair. Nothing is certain

L

about that mysterious writing, except that it was not made with the Dreyfus hand. The whole affair is a particularly striking example of that exasperating kind of historical event whereof more is known concerning what is false than what is true. It is simple enough to detect the fallacies; extremely difficult to isolate any indisputable fact from this morass of prejudice and perjury. Bertillon's supposed part in the disaster is an example. Many of the critics have put almost the whole weight of responsibility for the disaster upon his shoulders. This kind of criticism has been very generally accepted. It runs that Bertillon made a mistake and, having done so, was too obstinate and too vain to withdraw his original statement and save a man whom he knew to be innocent from life-long imprisonment. This, it is supposed, he should have done, when other more competent experts had declared that the hand-writing was not that of Dreyfus.

This is a monstrous reflection upon a man who, whatever his faults were, did not number a lack of integrity among them. It is quite true that a number of distinguished (and not so distinguished) experts made an investigation and found against Bertillon. What is not generally known is that not one of them had examined the original document. Some of the English and American examiners, at least, do not seem to have been aware that the reproduction they examined was an engraving. Even with the more refined methods now at our disposal, it is seldom possible to identify handwriting without an examination of the original, and never with certainty from an engraving.

But that they had not been in a position to examine the original document is a grave reflection upon the authorities who tried Dreyfus. At the Zola hearing, one of the most grotesquely dramatic trials in history, even the handwriting evidence had its share of drama. Labori and Albert Clemenceau, counsel for the Defence, demanded the production of the *bordereau*. The President of the Court ruled that this could not be done.

Couard, whom Zola had accused of being either insane or dishonest and of making fraudulent reports, went into the box. He was severely handled by Clemenceau.

So you say that the reproduction of the *bordereau* which our experts say is not in the handwriting of Dreyfus bears no resemblance whatever to the original. Is that what you tell the Court?

COUARD. Yes.

Well, if you have examined the original you can tell us precisely what the similarities and dissimilarities are.

COUARD. Yes, I can. The difference is that between two things which are not in the least alike.

LABORI. M. Couard, I suggest to you that there are no differences of any kind. What you are saying is that you have worked upon an entirely different document. Are you really telling Mr President and the Court that?

The witness said he was. It was his evidence that it was only by an examination of the original document that a conclusion could be reached, and his conclusion was that Dreyfus was the author of the *bordereau*.

Faced with the indefensible ruling that the original document could not be produced to them, the Defence fell back upon the only course open, which was to find evidence to show that the facsimile of this vital writing was at least accurate enough to form some opinion. Their witnesses were competent and honest, which is more than can be said for the lesser expert fry who gave evidence for the Prosecution.

Paul Meyer, director of the École des Chartes, Auguste Molinier, a professor there, and his brother, a distinguished curator of the Louvre Museum, were at one in their opinion that a good engraving faithfully reproduced the design of the original writing even if it obscured many details. With a shrewd thrust at the Prosecution Professor Molinier said that, since the reproduction of the *bordereau* had been published as evidence pointing to the guilt of Dreyfus, he hoped they believed it was a faithful reproduction. This was drawn from him by Clemenceau's skilful questioning in the teeth of the continued objections of the Prosecution. The professor was severely rebuked by the President of the Court for casting this oblique reflection on the good faith of Dreyfus's accusers. But the Prosecution was by this time in a difficult position. It could deny that it had actually sponsored the anti-Dreyfus publicity which had freely used the picture of the *bordereau* as evidence of the guilt of the accused, but in fact it had been released for publication. This implied that they thought it faithfully represented the original document.

The Defence brought up even heavier expert artillery in the person of Héricourt, a substantial authority upon palæography and written and printed texts generally. His evidence was that a good engraver could and did produce a faithful reproduction of his model, but the result was in some respects like that of good forgery, because the reproduction was a drawing without the spontaneity of natural handwriting. His evidence was an historical event, because it marked a definite stage of progress in the technical appreciation of handwriting movements which is the basis of modern expert technique.

Bertillon was in court, and, as shall be seen, he gave evidence. For the moment we are concerned not with his opinion upon the *bordereau,* but with his reactions to the witnesses who were with him in this disastrous matter. He had never associated himself with them, and he must have been a singularly unhappy man as he listened to their confused and incompetent evidence. No one knows what he thought of the Prosecution's tactics in refusing the Defence access to the document which had aroused such a furious controversy; no one knows what his opinion was of the expert evidence called by the Defence. This is not known, because, in the face of a campaign of slander and calumny wherein it was said that he was mad, that he was the cat's-paw of a tyrannical military clique, and an incompetent blunderer, he had maintained one of his characteristically cold and obstinate silences. This stony façade must have concealed an uncomfortable conviction that the Defence experts were at least honest men, competent to express an opinion. Quick to despise, and to recognize dishonesty, he must have known that the men associated with him by force of circumstances were no better than charlatans, who agreed with him not from informed conviction but because they thought it prudent to take what they believed to be the right side.

There would be no profit in considering in detail the wearisome and futile proceedings of the Court of Cassation of June 1899, but it did set aside the earlier judgment whereby Dreyfus was convicted of treason as the author of the *bordereau*, and ordered a new trial by court-martial at Rennes. The grotesque verdict of that court was "guilty with extenuating circumstances." After all, the accused was either guilty or not guilty, and, if guilty, there were no extenuating circumstances.

What is important is that Alfred Dreyfus was originally convicted on the evidence of the *bordereau* alone. There was no other. It was Bertillon who first examined that document, and it was he who found that Dreyfus had written it.

To begin with the Cassation proceedings is to reverse the sequence of the memorable story, but the evidence concerning the documents at this hearing provides the background in the light of which Bertillon's earlier part in it can be clarified. Because the *bordereau* was crucial, Dreyfus, who might have been convicted in spite of Bertillon's erroneous *expertise*, was convicted because of it. Nevertheless, for the sake of history no less than for the sake of the man whose biography is being written, it is necessary to be clear as to what, in fact, that mistake precisely was.

II

Because it has a bearing on the 'documents in the case' the background of this notorious affair must be enlarged. There is much ambiguity and mystery which has never been, and perhaps never can be, fully clarified. The accounts of the vital 'bordereau' itself are vague and conflicting, and, although the main facts concerning it are known, they have been so variously reported that the truth is difficult to appreciate. And it must be said again that everything depended upon that document. It was never shown when Captain Dreyfus was first arrested that there was any real evidence other than his handwriting to connect him with the *bordereau*, and, while it is true that other evidence was afterwards manufactured to bolster up the case against him, his innocence or guilt stood or fell in fact upon the identification of the handwriting.

Unless this is clear, it is impossible to arrive at any just appreciation of the facts.

Captain Alfred Dreyfus, an Alsatian Jew, and an artillery officer attached to the French General Staff, was arrested at the Ministry of War on October 15, 1894. While it is true that at that time France was in the grip of one of those periodical attacks of anti-Semitism which from time to time appear to infect individuals and peoples in other respects sane, it is quite untrue, as his supporters said, that he was suspected solely on account of his race. Because of his assertiveness and arrogance, Dreyfus was much disliked by many of his colleagues, but there is no evidence that any personal or racial prejudice influenced the Minister of War. It was the fatal *bordereau*. The arrest took place after a comparison had been made by a number of officers, two of whom professed some knowledge of handwriting. That the writing of the *bordereau* bears superficially a strong resemblance to that of Dreyfus is a fact often forgotten.

As is known well enough, the wording of the *bordereau* was such as to suggest that the document was the work of a traitor who was supplying or selling secret military information, particularly in connexion with artillery, to (presumably) the German Government. French fear of Germany had been increasing for some years, and it was very widely believed that it was German-Jewish influence which fostered the expansionist policy undeniably dominant in Germany at that time. This nerve-racked point of view encouraged precipitate and ill-advised action.

It was ill-advised, because no fully expert or informed opinion had been taken concerning the *bordereau* before the arrest was made. If there were ever a piece of writing which needed expert scrutiny the *bordereau* required it. The fact has been too little emphasized that it was written on both sides of *papier pelure*, the paper then used for foreign correspondence to save weight. This paper was thinner and even more translucent than our air-mail paper of to-day. The text was in many places obscured by the writing on the reverse side, which clearly showed through the paper. Also the document had been torn, not, as is generally reported, into small pieces but into four sections. With such an ambiguous clue in their hands, it might have been expected that more detailed examination would have been made before drastic action was taken.

The reason this was not done may well have been the distrust with which expert evidence regarding handwriting was—not without some reason—viewed in France and elsewhere at that time. It was then a principle of French, as of English, law that those most competent to give an opinion concerning the identity of a handwriting were individuals who "knew that handwriting well." This principle is not altogether unsound; but there exist so many cases where it does not apply that such evidence can never be conclusive, and it may be absolutely worthless. It must always be so if the specimen examined is not representative. Written upon paper of this kind, the *bordereau* was certainly not what document examiners call a standard writing.

The circumstances in which the *bordereau* was discovered are also generally known, but some unusual features surrounding the discovery do not seem to have been thought significant at the time. 'Intercepted' in September 1894 by an intelligence officer of the General Staff, the *bordereau* had been handed to Major Henry. It was said to have been on its way to Lieutenant-Colonel Schwartzkoppen, military attaché in Paris. No one seems to have remarked upon the singular fact that it was torn in four pieces.

Henry's confession, for what it was worth, made at a much later stage, provides an explanation of this. He is said to have declared that it was he who tore up the *bordereau*. Having recognized the handwriting as that of a friend of his, Major Walsin-Esterhazy, he had torn it up for fear of the consequences, and had only produced it under pressure from the agent who had handed it to him.

Whatever else may have been true or false in his confession, this extraordinary statement cannot survive critical examination. No sane man wishing to dispose of compromising evidence would have torn the paper in this way and retained the pieces. If, on the other hand, he feared to dispose of the *bordereau* by reason of the danger of being obliged to produce it his action is even less easily explained. It seems quite clear that, whatever the origin of the *bordereau* was, it was Henry's intention when he received it to pass it on to the *Deuxième Bureau*.

It is not possible to find the facts in this connexion. Quite simply it is not known whether the *bordereau* was a ' genuine ' document at all—genuine, that is to say, in the sense of being a bona-fide communication intended to give information to a foreign Power. It might as well be that the *bordereau* was nothing more than a scrap of paper originally fabricated and designed to frame Alfred Dreyfus or some other person unknown.

Although this should not be so, these considerations are of the very greatest significance because of their bearing upon the examination of the *bordereau* and the results of it. It is a lamentable fact that very few of the experts who examined the document, or some allegedly faithful reproduction of it, came to that investigation with an unbiased mind. They began their work with the conviction either that Dreyfus was innocent or that he was guilty. Those who were honest among them quite unconsciously made their technical finding conform to the pre-determined verdict. It is unnecessary to comment further upon the evidence of the witnesses who, with questionable motives, found what their clients wanted them to find.

It is now a well-established principle among competent examiners of questioned documents that beyond the sphere of information necessary to them to carry out the investigation they should believe nothing they hear and only half they see. Locard has brilliantly summarized the technical and ethical responsibilities imposed upon all bona-fide examiners of documents and handwriting. They must discourage the supply of, and in no circumstances seek, any information concerning the documents they examine, and must form a conclusion upon the physical facts alone. Having reached a conclusion, however, they may and should be informed of the surrounding circumstances. If these should seem to run contrary to their findings the technical evidence must then be carefully reviewed.

This may be a counsel of perfection, difficult to apply fully in every case; but in the very circumstances it could have been

applied to the *Affaire Dreyfus.* There would then have been
no *Affaire Dreyfus,* no political bitterness, no riots, no
imprisonment of a man not proved guilty.

This is not to say that a definite conclusion could have
been reached in the first place or that the conclusions ultimately arrived at, after so much damage had been done, were
necessarily the right ones. All that need have happened in the
interests of justice was that both sides should have agreed that
no definite conclusion was possible on the technical evidence
before them. It is quite a mistake to suppose that even with
the greatly improved technical methods available to us to-day
it is always possible to decide the identity of a handwriting or
in all cases to be able to declare positively whether a given
piece of writing is or is not forged. This is no reflection upon
the methods employed for the examination of questioned
documents or upon the compétence of those who use them.
On the contrary, this cautious approach is a safeguard and an
awful warning against ignorant rashness which can defeat the
ends of justice. The *Affaire Dreyfus* is a striking and exceptionally shocking example of the results of expressing positive
opinions in excess of those warranted by the facts.

Not the least tragic aspect of the affair was the undoubted
good faith of the original accusers of Dreyfus. In the heat of
controversy it was said, and it is said still, that Mercier
pursued the prosecution of Dreyfus, knowing him to be
innocent. The drive behind this accusation, as of most others
at that time, was political prejudice. It does not square with
Mercier's character and record. However blind and obstinate,
it is unjust to question his good faith. He was alone in his
refusal to endorse the ultimate decision of the Chamber to
exonerate Dreyfus and restore his military rank. His words do
not suggest that he was trying to deceive others, even if he
were deceiving himself :

" My conscience, gentlemen, I say again, my conscience,
will not allow me to endorse this verdict. . . ."

He was not alone in this scruple. There were others who
thought as he did even if they remained silent. This disposes
of the assertion, of which his critics made so much, that
Bertillon was the sole occupant of the last anti-Dreyfus ditch,

and that he obstinately defended the accuracy of his *expertise* in the face of an unanimous opinion to the contrary.

III

" My name," said a man who came to visit Bertillon, probably not more than a week after the arrest of Dreyfus, " is Gobert. I understand you may be able to help me with photographs—enlargements? "

" Perhaps; but what enlargements? "

" Documents—a document."

In this unremarkable fashion the drama of the Dreyfus case began. Requests of this kind reached his department frequently. Bertillon's photographic work was well known for its quality, and it had become almost standard practice to approach him when this work had to be done. Since he was often asked for help by other departments than those of the police, he was not surprised to learn that his visitor was an expert attached to the Bank of France for the examination of banknotes.

" I must know," said Bertillon, " for what purpose these enlargements are required if they are to be of satisfactory service to you."

Gobert, a professionally cautious man, hesitated.

" It is a very delicate matter, M. Bertillon."

This was not the right way to deal with Bertillon. The indirect approach always exasperated him.

" Do you think, M. Gobert, that it is only the Bank of France which has to deal with delicate matters? I am the Chief of the Department of Judicial Identity, and I resent having my discretion questioned."

Perhaps no one but Bertillon could have construed so reasonable a remark in such a way. Gobert, uncomfortable and much taken aback, nevertheless gave Bertillon the facts.

" You have heard of the arrest of Captain Alfred Dreyfus? "

" No."

He listened carefully to Gobert's recital and learnt that the evidence leading to the arrest was the disclosure to the *Deuxième Bureau* of a document called the *bordereau*. A number of intelligence officers had examined it, among them

Lieutenant-Colonel Paty de Clam, who was an amateur of graphology. Colonel d'Abbeville had also been particularly struck with the resemblance of the writing to that of Dreyfus. General Mercier was not satisfied, and had insisted that the document must go to an expert. He had done this on the advice of Guérin, Keeper of the Seals. Guérin, who was a distinguished and trusted Minister, was a member of the select committee which Mercier had appointed to advise him. It was Guérin who had named Gobert.

" I have examined the document and told them that I was not at all satisfied that the writing was that of Dreyfus." [Le bordereau paraît être d'une autre personne que celle soupçonnée.]

Bertillon was sceptical. He had no belief in the effectiveness of handwriting as a means of identifying the person. Graphology, by which is understood the psychological interpretation of handwriting, he absolutely repudiated.

But it has been said that he was impressed with Gobert's very commendable caution, and he was quite willing to undertake the photographic work, which in any case was regarded as one of the responsibilities of his department.

This is the manner whereby Bertillon was introduced to the writing which was politically and socially to rend France in twain. That he first sought to examine the document, and considered himself competent to deal with the problem of the identification of the writing, is a legend which was invented by his opponents without the slightest basis in fact. The circumstances which caused him later to undertake the *expertise* are not directly known, but they can be reconstructed with a very high degree of probability.

Bertillon's system of classifying and grouping writings was founded upon the one he had developed in his anthropometric system. This relied, first of all, upon measurement. There is no doubt that as a matter of routine he had treated the *bordereau* in the same way. First, however, he had noted the significant fact that it was written upon *papier pelure*, an unusual circumstance which had immediately attracted his attention. He was later to say in court what he undoubtedly inferred at the time :

The *bordereau* is on *pelure*. It is unusual for letters to be written on paper of this sort unless the volume of the correspondence is large and would incur a high postal charge. Here there is only one sheet. The use of this paper thus suggests that the writing might have been traced.

Bertillon's whole *expertise* was developed on the basis of this perfectly fair inference from the original fact. It explains how, with all his distrust of the techniques of handwriting identification, he was prepared to undertake the examination. The problem to be solved was not so much the direct identification of the writer, which he rejected as impossible, as to expose the method whereby, if fabricated, the writing had been made.

It was upon this basis that he developed his thesis concerning the *bordereau*. The technical work that he did in an attempt to find further facts which might support this preliminary conclusion was beyond reproach.

Bertillon was not a man who readily co-operated with others, but in this case he was isolated as much by circumstances as by choice. The matter was highly confidential, and he would have been obliged in any case to keep it to himself. But he could have co-operated with Gobert, in whom he had great confidence. In his *Comparison of Writings*, which he published in the *Revue Scientifique* in 1898, Bertillon went out of his way to name Gobert as a competent authority upon the examination of documents, and as " a distinguished chemist." This was high praise from a man who was not lavish in this respect.

There is little doubt that he would have worked with Gobert had there been an opportunity of doing so, and had they attacked the problem together it is likely enough that the history of the Dreyfus Affair would have been different. The truth is that Gobert was determined not to become involved in the matter. Even at that early stage he evidently thought that there might be far-reaching consequences.

Bertillon was in a difficult position. He had been officially invited, if not instructed, to examine the *bordereau*. Gobert had been deputed to request him to take photographs of the document. The bank official was not committed to continue an examination which he quite evidently wished to avoid. Even if he had wished to do so Bertillon could not, in these circumstances, seek his co-operation.

This is a very different picture of the situation from that made out at the time. It was commonly said—and even many of Bertillon's supporters believed it—that he had undertaken the work at his own request, and believed that he was suitably qualified to complete it.

Whether in this instance he preferred to work alone or not, he had no choice. Isolated with his problem, he became pre-occupied and almost obsessed by it. The defects of Bertillon's formal education made his *a priori* judgments very dangerous and edged tools. His first and not unreasonable conclusion was that the writing he had to examine was traced. This placed it outside the conventional methods of *expertise* for the identification of handwriting, the validity of which he always doubted. Methods of measurement which he had so brilliantly applied in another field might throw light upon the problem and confirm or dispose of his first conclusion.

After the event it is, of course, very easy to appreciate the dangers of the *a priori* approach to a problem of this kind, but Bertillon was not the first man of high intelligence and of scientific habit of mind to formulate a theory and then to seek and to find experimental evidence which seems to confirm it.

The facts he so meticulously sought and found were of a very interesting character. Again, this is what he said in evidence:

> Certain recurring words and certain syllables appearing many times in the text are identical with each other. In a spontaneous writing no two words ever show this correspondence. Here there are many. This confirms the conclusion that the writing is a tracing.

By 'identical' he meant not so much the design of the characters but the actual length of a number of words and syllables. This was shown by superimposing parallel equidistant lines indicating the manner whereby like words and syllables corresponded in dimension.

Similarly, in the spacing, Bertillon found that a space corresponding to 1.25 millimetres or a multiple of this measurement continually recurred throughout the writing. The conclusion he drew from these facts was that, first, the tracing had been produced from a model upon which was superimposed a scale, and that, secondly, the scale was divided at intervals of 1.25 millimetres. What was then sometimes known as a ' Kutsch ' is divided in this way, and it was used in the scaling of military maps. The *bordereau* was thus produced by a person familiar with this type of scale, and thus with military maps—namely, a staff officer.

It was at this logical point of departure that Bertillon began his perilous journey whereon he lost himself in a maze of speculation. So arose his identification of the word *intérêt* in a note written by Mathieu Dreyfus, the brother of Alfred, with the *bordereau* writing. This conclusion was founded upon the discovery that it had the metrical characteristics such that it could have served as a model for the tracing of the *bordereau*. The spacing of the strokes corresponded to 1.25 millimetres or an exact multiple of this figure, and its total length was an exact multiple of it. By this dangerously speculative method Bertillon proved to his own entire satisfaction that the questioned writing was a tracing of an unique character. The object was not to reproduce an imitation of the design, but to disguise the writing by imposing upon it metrical relationships not found in the natural hand.

It would be very easy to dismiss this theoretical build-up, not only as rash, but frankly unsound if it were not for a method 'of demonstration which Bertillon used at the trial. That the Military Court at Rennes did not understand Bertillon's exposition of this complicated hypothesis is not surprising. He was nervous, unaccustomed to giving evidence, and, in the most favourable circumstances, a poor expositor. But they understood his excellent photographs and the demonstration which accompanied them. It must have been a dramatic moment when Bertillon with the aid of a five-centime piece, a sheet of translucent paper, and a pencil actually ' fabricated ' an excellent imitation of the *bordereau* by the method of tracing he had so dismally failed verbally to describe. The function of the five-centime piece was its size, since the diameter of the coin of that time was 2.5 centimetres, which is an exact multiple (20 times) of 1.25 millimetres.

It was this demonstration and not Bertillon's evidence itself which impressed the court, but it is perhaps less surprising that it should finally have convinced Bertillon himself. By this means he had experimentally proved that what he called an auto-forgery could be produced by this method. There would have been no fallacy if Bertillon had contented himself with the conclusion that the facts he so conscientiously exposed indicated with a high degree of probability the method whereby the questioned wording had been produced. He might even have gone further in suggesting that it was a fair inference that this elaborate method of disguise was consistent with an author having a military and mathematical background.

This would have been to stretch valid inference to its limits. What is less easy to understand is that, having arrived at this point, Bertillon at once overreached it. His final conclusion was that these facts were consistent with only one author, and that author was Alfred Dreyfus.

To be quite just to him, this was not the only evidence upon which he relied. It is an interesting fact not commonly known that Bertillon's preliminary examination of the *bordereau* caused him at first to form the same opinion as Gobert. He noted and remarked upon a number of significant differences between the standard writing of Dreyfus and the questioned writing. It was the facts which seemed to point to an artificial method of producing the writing which caused him to change his opinion. He attributed the differences to the artifice of auto-forgery. The resemblances (which certainly exist in fact) were due to the natural characteristics of the writing which the forger could not suppress. This does not explain how it came about that he seemed to have renounced his principle that it was impossible positively to identify the person by an examination of his handwriting which stemmed from the extreme caution and objectivity normally characteristic of him in such matters.

The causes of this change must be sought in the special

circumstances and their reaction upon Bertillon's social and individual psychology. When first approached by General Mercier, he refused to undertake the *expertise*. It was only after it had been represented to him that where the safety of France was concerned it was his duty to co-operate that he reluctantly consented.

Bertillon was by tradition a Liberal, and, although obliged to pay lip-service to Protestantism in his youth, his theological bias, if he had any, was Catholic. In principle he was anti-Semitic, but he was not so in practice. He had a great regard for his sister-in-law, the wife of his brother Jacques. She was of a Polish family and partly Jewish.

In spite of his international reputation and connexions Bertillon was that type of Frenchman who was wholly devoted to his country. The excellent virtue of patriotism in its real and true sense was a highly developed element in his character. It may be evident from what has already been written of him here that he was a man who was dangerously liable to carry both his virtues and vices to excess. So it was with his patriotism. He could lecture his family and his friends upon the biological decline of France and her need for re-generation. It was a subject upon which he had a very limited knowledge but the most pronounced opinion. He could scarify French policy and French politicians, but in a last resort it was his country, right or wrong.

A (so to call it) strong social orientation is as common among scientific men as among others. The difficulty is that in some circumstances it can be much more dangerous to them than to the man in the street. In his ordinary professional work Bertillon's social conscience could inspire but could not, even subconsciously, prejudice his findings. In the Dreyfus Affair it was his misfortune to be faced with a situation particularly dangerous to a man with a social conscience orientated as his was. Locard, who was his pupil and life-long friend and who knew him as well as anyone knew Bertillon, has put the matter in a nutshell in his brilliant summary of the Bertillon attitude in this:

I have had a number of conversations with Alphonse Bertillon on this matter. I cannot claim that I had his full

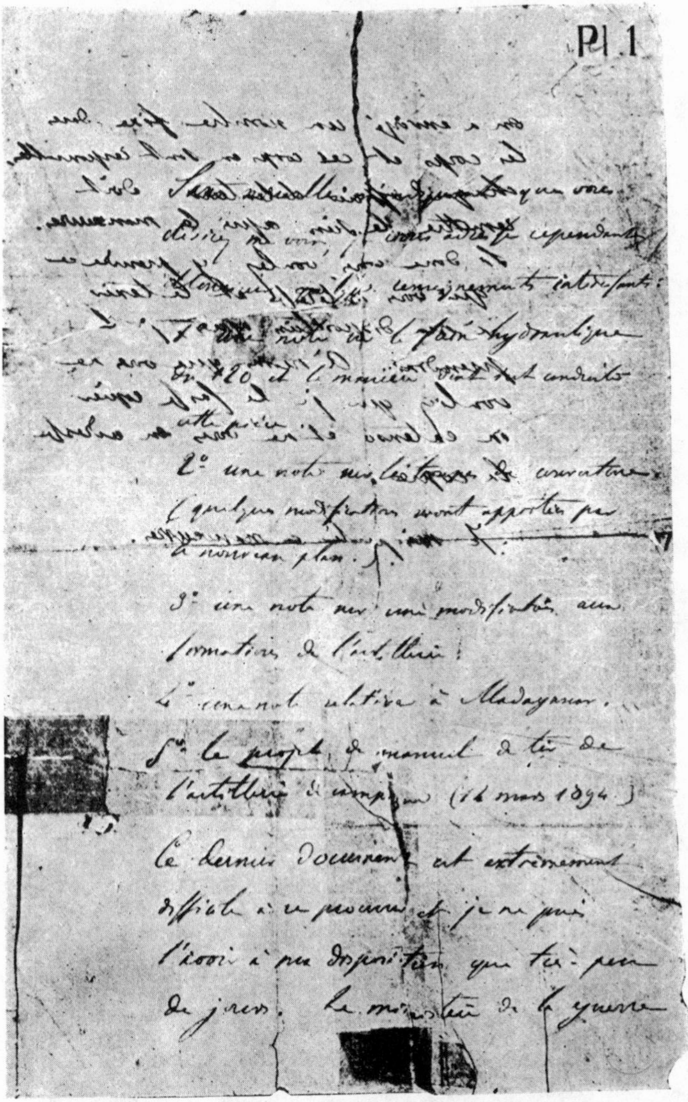
Pl. 1

Sans nouvelles m'indiquant que vous
désirez me voir, je vous adresse cependant
Monsieur, quelques renseignements intéressants:

1° une note sur le frein hydraulique
du 120 et la manière dont s'est conduite
cette pièce;

2° une note sur les troupes de couverture
(quelques modifications seront apportées par
le nouveau plan).

3° une note sur une modification aux
formations de l'artillerie.

4° une note relative à Madagascar.

5° le projet de manuel de tir de
l'artillerie de campagne (14 mars 1894.)

Ce dernier document est extrêmement
difficile à se procurer et je ne puis
l'avoir à ma disposition que très peu
de jours. Le ministère de la guerre

The Only Certainly Authentic Photograph of the "Bordereau" in its Original Condition

[handwritten text in French cursive]

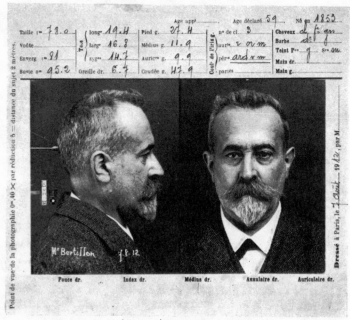

"HOIST WITH HIS OWN PETARD"
Bertillon photographed by his own anthropometric method.

confidence. That would be an exaggeration for many reasons and principally because self-revelation was not a habit of his. But I think that it is no betrayal of him to say that he believed as others of his ' party '[1] did—if one must use this word— that he was serving his country as well as the cause of justice. ' Service '[1] is too feeble a word. It was a question of saving his country.

This is not the place to pursue that, except so far as it shows how these circumstances conspired to make Bertillon accept an *expertise* which he ought to have refused. He was informed, most improperly, but in perfectly good faith, that there was already evidence concerning the authorship of the *bordereau* which pointed to Dreyfus. The only standards of comparison submitted to him were in the first place those of Dreyfus. Bertillon, sceptical, as well he might be, of the technical methods applied to the examination of handwriting at that time, found applicable (as he thought) in this special case a technique with which he was familiar, and by which he discovered a number of significant facts. That he drew inferences in excess of what these facts justified is a verdict very different from that of his traducers, who branded him as a blunderer or a madman.

IV

Alfred Dreyfus, arrested in October 1894, was tried in Paris on December 19 of the same year by a Military Court sitting *in camera*. He was found guilty, sentenced to dismissal with ignominy and imprisonment for life. The sentence was carried out in January 1895. It is a remarkable and significant fact that the matter attracted no attention at the time. It has been said that towards the end of 1897 Léon Blum was told that Dreyfus was innocent. He could not at first even remember the name, but he subsequently recollected that an officer attached to the General Staff had, in fact, been tried and convicted for treason. It evidently had not occurred to him, or to anyone of note, that the verdict was suspect. The circumstances were that the trial had been held *in camera*, and no complete report of it had ever been issued. Although the accused had been represented by Counsel, the lawyer had been

1 The inverted commas are mine.

warned that any disclosure of the evidence was a penal offence.

Thus the details of the first evidence given by Bertillon are known only by inference. It is, however, quite certain that he began his examination of the *bordereau* in October, and that he had two months at least to complete his work. There is no reason to believe that the evidence he gave at that time differed substantially from that which he repeated subsequently.

The circumstances which led up to the sensational reopening of the matter are too well known to require detailed repetition; but there is a fact in this connexion which stands out and must be noted. Lieutenant-Colonel Georges Picquart, who became Chief of Intelligence in July 1895, was an anti-Semite; but, as his actions were to show, he was a just and honourable man. The first trial convinced him of the guilt of Dreyfus. Whether this was due to the handwriting evidence or to that of Colonel Henry, who then enjoyed the full confidence of the military authorities, is not known; but it indicates quite clearly that there was no conspiracy to convict an innocent man.

The clue which first raised grave doubts in Picquart's mind was the discovery of the notorious *petit bleu*. This document was stated to have been found torn in small pieces [1] in a wastepaper basket in the German Embassy in Paris by a French agent. If this were in fact true it seems to suggest a lack of thoroughness, supposed not to be characteristic of the Germans, concerning their security methods. However that may be, there is no doubt that the *petit bleu* came into Picquart's hands and that it implicated Major Walsin-Esterhazy in the crime of supplying information to the German authorities. Picquart accordingly compared the writing of the *bordereau* with that of Esterhazy and reached the conclusion

---

[1] In respect of the manner of its destruction, this document is often confused with the *bordereau* itself. I myself have made this mistake, as a reference to page 74 of *In the Tracks of Crime* will show. Dr Locard informed me that the *bordereau* was, in fact, torn in four pieces. I have since seen a reproduction of the original photograph, taken by Bertillon, which is the only accurate record of the *bordereau* which exists. Although there is subsidiary damage, it seems clear that it was originally torn in four.

that he was the author of the document which Dreyfus had
been accused and convicted of writing.

There is one question of which there is no possible doubt.
It is that Major Walsin-Esterhazy was a cold-blooded and unscrupulous villain. Said to be a cadet of the famous Hungarian
family, with some Jewish blood, he was a traitor, with a
financial interest in treason, and a man who would stop at
nothing if he saw monetary advantage in it.

This began the furious battle of the Dreyfusards and anti-
Dreyfusards, in which were embroiled the handwriting experts
whether they liked it or not. Whatever the defects of Bertillon's *expertise*—and on analysis they are obvious enough—his
work compares only too favourably with that produced by the
opposing side. This is not to question the at least moderate
competence of much of the *contra-expertise* and the honesty
of a good deal of it. But its value as evidence is reduced
almost to vanishing point because of one central fact which
was vital as far as the document examination was concerned.
Not one of them, as has been said, had examined the original
document, and most, if not all, had based their reports upon
an inaccurate reproduction of the original. This is a disgrace-
ful reflection upon the methods whereby the Prosecution conducted its case once a doubt had been thrown upon the verdict
of the first military court which convicted Dreyfus in
December 1894. It has been stated on good authority that no
expert, even for the Prosecution—except Bertillon—ever had
an opportunity of making detailed examination of the
bordereau, and that it was released to him only with great
reluctance because he refused to make a report unless full
access to the document was given to him.

By the same token, the experts for the Defence might reason-
ably have refused to give any opinion concerning the questioned writing. In the circumstances it would be unfair to
suggest that this was ethically required of them, but the truth
is that many of them expressed positive opinions which were
quite unjustified having regard to the material at their disposal. Nor was their initial approach likely to have been more
objective than Bertillon's. They already knew that there was
a grave doubt concerning the authorship of the *bordereau*,

and most, if not all, were aware that Esterhazy was thought to be the writer of it.

There were exceptions who, with commendable caution, produced reports which were of greater value, precisely because they did not assume too much or enlarge upon the available evidence. Rougemont, a distinguished expert at that time in France, in a guarded opinion said that he could not absolutely reject the theory that the writing of the *bordereau* was simulated. Thomas Henry Gurrin, father of a distinguished handwriting expert still in practice in London, expressed this opinion:

> By a simulated writing, I mean the writing of a person obliged to imitate the writing of some other person. I can prove my assertion that the document attributed to Captain Dreyfus is not a disguised but simulated writing. My opinion is that the person who wrote this document tried to imitate some of the characteristics of the writing of Captain Dreyfus, but he has not succeeded very well.

Gustave Bridier, more speculative, is less convincing. He thought the handwriting abnormal on account of the heavy shading and the hesitancy noticeable in many of the strokes. There was a lack of " unity " in it, which suggested that it might have been constructed from various originals which had formed the model for the fabricated document.

The opinion of the distinguished Crépieux-Jamin is perhaps the most significant of all. This dentist, who became at the same time a renowned student of handwriting, was a graphologist. Whatever we may think of the psychology of handwriting which Jamin professed, it remains true that the empirical evidence he patiently collected cannot be ignored; and the less so in this case because his psychological interpretation of handwriting did not necessarily require the examination of the original. After a characteristically careful and conscientious examination, Jamin came to the conclusion that the writing was not that of Dreyfus.

Even the handwriting experts in those stirring times stood in need of heroic qualities. Crépieux-Jamin had the misfortune to number many anti-Dreyfusards among his friends and clients. When his findings became known the windows of his house were smashed, his friends refused to acknowledge him in the street, and his clients in fear of their lives and limbs forsook him. Unmoved and uncomplaining, he persisted in making his findings known to all those whom he thought ought to be acquainted with them. Bertillon was not alone in paying a high price in adhering to an opinion honestly held and consistently maintained in the face of threats and violence.

The significance of the evidence is that on balance the best-informed technical opinion was not incompatible with the findings which, on the facts he so conscientiously exposed, Bertillon ought to have arrived at—namely, that the questioned writing was a simulated writing.

Bertillon, on the contrary, not only maintained but enlarged his thesis at the Military Court at Rennes. At that trial he utilized a statistical proof to show that the correspondence found in like words and syllables of the *bordereau* established as a matter of fact that the writings had been traced by the method he had described. What the demonstration proved was its author's very uncertain grasp of the principles of the calculus of probability. It impressed those members of the court who were without mathematical background. The technically trained officers shrugged. Later Poincaré, the mathematician, was to demolish the insecure structure once and for all. The Bertillon mathematics were not non-existent; he understood the more or less elementary probability equations applicable to his anthropometric system, but he had achieved this by the empirical methods of which he was a past master. His mind, unattuned to the mathematical discipline which he would have acquired had his education been more systematic, had no grasp of mathematical generalizations or ability to apply them correctly in practice.

It may have been a like defect in his intellectual equipment which made him fall back upon another device to clarify his thesis which really did produce laughter in court. It was the famous *Redan, ou Citadelle des Rébus Graphiques.* This diagram purported to show schematically the means whereby the forger of the *bordereau* had protected himself from any chance of exposure or attack either from the right or the left.

As a method of clarifying his always turgid exposition it was not a success; but the taunts of his adversaries that it proved him mad were gross libel upon him. This unfortunate document was nothing worse than an abortive attempt to translate into non-technical symbols what was in fact an over-elaborated piece of technical evidence.

V

On January 13, 1898, appeared Zola's famous letter *J'Accuse*. Two hundred thousand copies were sold, and it created so violent a disturbance that the leading Socialist, Guesde, called it the most significant revolutionary gesture of the century. It appeared two days after the acquittal of the rascally Esterhazy, who had submitted to a mock trial designed to clear him of suspicion of being the author of the *bordereau*. In this letter Zola indicted the three experts for the Defence and accused them, not without reason, of perjured evidence. Whether or not they believed that the writing of the *bordereau* was not that of Esterhazy is irrelevant. What is certain is that they were retained by the Defence to give a gloss of technical respectability to the prearranged verdict of acquittal, and they played the part which was expected of them. The thunder of Zola's accusations really did produce a near-revolutionary situation. Serious rioting became fairly frequent. University students, who always became obstreperous on such occasions, beat up their professors, according as their sympathies lay, and then, for the sake of variety, beat up each other.

It is doubtful if Esterhazy's ultimate confession that he was in fact the author of the *bordereau*—made from the shelter of the other side of the Channel—convinced anyone at the time unless they were already converted. Convinced anti-Dreyfusards believed that the confession was false and had been made because it was in some way to the advantage of this slippery Hungarian. The air was thick with rumour. There was one widely circulated to the effect that a woman, a Drey-fusard, on hearing from his own lips that he intended to publish his confession in a French newspaper, said, " Esterhazy, you are an angel." The inference was that there was a conspiracy. Esterhazy, with nothing to lose since he had escaped from

France, was (so they said) quite willing to make a 'confession' for a suitable consideration. In the case of a dog with so bad a name, nothing was easier than to defend assertions of this kind, because they may so well have been true.

These sensational developments, far from clarifying the murky atmosphere and uniting opinion, aggravated the conflict between the partisans. It separated friends and disunited families. It even embroiled intellectuals, like Proust, who could no longer ignore the conflict, however determined they might be to escape from it. He spoke for many in his sombre lament that there were no friendships now but political ones.

More directly to our purpose is the fact that it split the Bertillon clan. Jacques and Alphonse Bertillon had always been closely united from their boyhood's days. Alphonse Bertillon was not a good or voluminous correspondent, but the great majority of his letters which survive were written to his brother Jacques. They are not effusive or affectionate, for this was not in accordance with his character; but they all reflect the solid friendship which was between the two.

When Colonel Henry's forgeries, which had been deliberately designed to bolster up the case against Dreyfus, came to light Jacques Bertillon became a Dreyfusard. Despite what has been reported, it is not certain that Henry's confession convinced him. It would have taken more than the admissions of a self-confessed liar to convince an anti-Dreyfusard that Henry's confession finally disposed of the charge that Dreyfus was the author of the *bordereau*. The more moderate of them must have admitted that it was true that Henry had subsequently forged documents more fully to implicate Dreyfus. The evidence was overwhelming. But it was never suggested that he had forged the *bordereau*. The report was that when it had come into his hands he had 'recognized' the writing of Esterhazy. He had then torn the document in four pieces and retained it, fearing to dispose of it altogether. Unsupported, it is not a convincing story, and the anti-Dreyfusards were logically entitled to make the most of it.

More probably the truth is that Jacques Bertillon never was a convinced anti-Dreyfusard and that his position became increasingly difficult as the affair took on, more and more, the clear-cut features of a pro-Semitic and anti-Semitic conflict. His wife, after all, had Jewish blood. Nothing is more probable than that the Henry sensation provided an escape, however difficult, from a painful dilemma.

Alphonse Bertillon took the change of front badly. The breach between them was never entirely healed. After having been in his youth a rebel and a prodigal, he became a devoted client of the Bertillon tradition that blood was much thicker than water. The Dreyfus Affair did not separate him from his friends. Lacassagne, frank and hard-hitting, who could say to him, " Bertillon, vous avez des rides en oméga; vous êtes un constipé," without giving him the slightest offence was a Dreyfusard and had held that conviction from the beginning. They could agree to differ, but that Jacques, his brother, who had supported him, should surrender to the enemy was almost more than he could bear. This was an immeasurably heavier blow than the savage and venomous campaign of calumny and slander of which he was made the principal target. Thus, for example, Joseph Reinach, a distinguished man in his fashion, and ordinarily a just one, wrote :

> In a man who in ordinary life was honest and disinterested one must look for the motive of such a terrible obsession; it was nothing more than a monstrous *amour propre*. At any price he must get the better of the Jews and journalists who had held him up to public ridicule. It is not only a question of madness evident in his wild eye, his gestures of a maniac or an enraged puppet, and his raucous voice such as is heard when the insane leave their cells; it is rather a matter of that kind of insanity wherein what remains of lucidity becomes a mechanism responding only to one stimulus and incapable of common rational judgment while at the same time it retains a certain astuteness, cunning, and deceit.

This is a fair sample of the more moderate kind of criticisms of which Bertillon was one of the principal objects. He did not, of course, suffer alone. Language like this was at that time the daily currency of both Dreyfusard and anti-Dreyfusard.

It is at least to his credit that he never attempted to repay his critics in so base a currency. In those hours of darkness he used, as a matter of duty, to read these hysterical polemics. If in a restrained and not very obvious fashion he was a masochist believing himself a martyr for France, at least he maintained the rôle with dignity. The only comment he made upon Reinach's outburst was characteristic : " Reinach is a man of intelligence. Until now, I have always believed him to be without passion or hatred and one who should pass for a generous opponent."

The Dreyfus Affair was Bertillon's Waterloo, and in that campaign he received wounds from which he never recovered. He entered the battle voluntarily, but equipped with weapons which were in no sense properly adapted to their purpose. He lacked altogether the kind of character and qualifications necessary in the witness-box. He was no Orfila, Lacassagne, or Bernard Spilsbury. Had his *expertise* in the Dreyfus case been as sound and complete as, in·fact, he thought it was it would still have failed to convince any properly constituted court. It was not his *métier*. The fact that he was almost certainly aware of this only makes the catastrophe the greater.

It remains to try to extract from a confused and almost chaotic picture such elements as may make it possible to interpret it. Most, if not all, of them are of a negative character.

Despite the confessions of Esterhazy and Henry, which are often accepted as final, there is no conclusive evidence concerning the authorship of the *bordereau*. As evidence, the confessions, if not worthless, are so highly suspect as to be quite inacceptable in terms of formal proof.

In regard to the technical evidence, owing to the advantages that Bertillon enjoyed in having full access to the original document, the technique of his *expertise* was more efficient than any other. It is probable, but not certain, that his finding that the document, or part of it, was produced by a method of tracing was justified, although his attempts to establish formal proof of it were invalid.

If he was correct in this it would have been impossible conclusively to identify the writer of the *bordereau* by an examination of the handwriting. Bertillon's gravest error was that by exposing the method whereby the document had been produced he concluded that he had exposed the identity of the writer. That a man who had discovered and laid down the first principles relating to the identity of the person should have made this mistake remains inexplicable.

Since there was no evidence, as far as is known, other than the handwriting of the *bordereau* upon which the accused could have been convicted, and since the evidence of the handwriting was, in the circumstances of the case, inconclusive, it follows that the conviction of Alfred Dreyfus for treason is among the worst miscarriages of justice in European history.

It is consoling that past errors often contribute to scientific and technical revelation. We owe, for example, to Bertillon the initiation of a technique which, though he incorrectly applied it, can now be utilized in some cases for the identification of handwriting, a process in the validity of which he did not believe. It is also an ironic reflection upon his scepticism that the process he formulated has in fact been applied for the purpose of overthrowing the conclusions he arrived at in the Dreyfus case. As a result of the development of his technique of the measurement of handwriting it has since his time been shown that the metrical characteristics of some handwritings, but by no means all, are of such a character as positively to identify them.

Some years ago our colleague Chevassus, at the Laboratories of Technical Police of the Prefecture of the Rhône, made a metrical comparison in respect of proportional size and angular values of the handwritings of Dreyfus, Esterhazy, and the questioned writing of the *bordereau*. This examination revealed the fact that there was a closer correspondence in these values between the handwriting of the *bordereau* and that of Esterhazy than was shown by the comparison of the Dreyfus writing with that of the *bordereau*. He accordingly concluded that the questioned writing was, in fact, that of Esterhazy.

It is doubtful if this interesting analysis can be accepted as conclusive. First, if the writing, or any part of it, is a tracing the results have no significance, since a traced forgery clearly will not show the metrical characteristics of the undisguised hand. Secondly, like the unfortunate experts for the Defence, Chevassus was obliged to use reproductions taken from the

works of Lazare and Reinach. The accuracy of these reproductions is doubtful.

The Dreyfus Affair, whose reverberations have not entirely
died away even to this day, still remains an unsolved problem.
We cannot and perhaps never shall be able with complete confidence to answer the question—who wrote the *bordereau*?

PART FOUR

POST HOC SED PROPTER HOC

22. COLLEAGUES

IN the opinion of his critics, Bertillon's reputation never recovered from the Dreyfus Affair. This is not borne out by the dates of the decorations conferred upon him. In all, he received fourteen distinctions, and of these seven date from a period after Zola's open letter, *J'Accuse*. In August 1898 he became a Knight of the Order of Königlichen Kronen of Germany, a Knight of the Order of Dannebrog of Denmark in March 1902, an Officer of the Order of the Star of Roumania in the same year, a Knight of the Order of St Maurice and St Lazare of Italy in 1908, a Commander of the Order in 1913, and a Commander of the Order of Isabella the Catholic of Spain in 1913.

Abroad, where opinion was unclouded by political prejudices, it was possible to pass an objective judgment upon his work as a whole, and these awards are evidence that the verdict was not only favourable but expressive of the great contributions he had made to the science of identification, and the profound social significance of his discoveries.

Bertillon had little interest in such things in themselves. He is said to have valued two things less intrinsically valuable than the Stars and Orders. For reasons which shall presently appear he received a photograph of the Duke of Windsor, then Prince of Wales, in 1912, which he greatly prized. His *Drummond Castle* medal also had a place of honour. The more elaborate pieces were not displayed.

The kind of reward Bertillon most appreciated was a personal understanding of and sympathy with his work, and he might have secured this in much fuller measure if his intense reserve had not made personal contact difficult. He never went abroad; he seldom left Paris; he did not 'mix.' If anyone wanted to see Bertillon they had to come to the

Prefecture, climb the innumerable stairs, and hope for the best. His critics interpreted this as the worst kind of pride; his friends and those who recognized the quality of his achievement knew better, and did not confuse his remote diffidence with conceit.

His first meeting with Louis Pasteur is an example of one of his rare successes in personal contact. It was probably in 1889. Pasteur, a man then approaching seventy, sought Bertillon out. Neither had had a formal scientific education; both had had great obstacles to overcome in the struggle for recognition; so that perhaps each had at once instinctively recognized a natural ally in the other. However that may be, Pasteur seems to have been one of the few who won Bertillon's confidence immediately.

The great biochemist listened carefully to his exposition of the essentials of the anthropometric system, which Bertillon found clearer words to explain than was often the case with him. Afterwards he expressed astonishment at the great psychological penetration which he thought inspired Pasteur's first question, as if there were something almost miraculous in it :

" That is very clear. Did you have much difficulty in convincing the administrative authorities of the value of your discovery? "

Under suitable stimulus Bertillon could be eloquent. This was the stimulus required. With an expansiveness uncommon to him, he told Pasteur the history of his life and, not only that, the history of his family as well. The whole is significantly summed up in the last words.

" You see, I come of a proud and obstinate family who when they are convinced of something which is right and just pursue it, and particularly if it seems to have a social value."

This exposes as clearly as anything could the motives which inspired Bertillon, but which from an almost morbid fear of committing himself he found so difficult to express. It seems to have made a considerable impression upon Pasteur. They were friends from that day. Pasteur was not to live to see the hours of darkness which the Dreyfus case produced. He died a year after the arrest of Dreyfus and before the controversy arose.

It is an interesting fact that a pile of visiting-cards, preserved by the family and now in the keeping of Dr François Bertillon, provides significant evidence concerning those who sought Bertillon out in the almost monastic seclusion of his office for good or indifferent motives. Typographically they often speak for themselves. There is the card of the discomfited Vucetich —a little obtrusive, with typographical flourishes, as are many of the South American cards. A number of the Italians and Central Europeans liked to print almost a précis of their life's history beneath their names. The Germans and the Scandinavians are neater and more restrained. American cards, expensively printed, range from the merely blatant to the super-refined. The English examples, least obtrusive and most standardized of all, are, on the whole, the best printed. There is one, in particular—a beautifully engraved copper-plate. The only printed words upon it are the name—Mr Francis Galton.

On the card is written, presumably in the owner's handwriting, " Vendredi vers 2¼ heures avant grand désir de voir vos appareils photographiques."

There is no other clue, but there can be no doubt that he saw the photographic apparatus on the Friday. Francis Galton was one of the people whom Bertillon would have seen even without an appointment. He was in no way influenced by the fact that the great English anthropologist had originally been an advocate of his system, but in that year (1892) had reached the conclusion that fingerprints were to be preferred to anthropometric measurements.

It is unlikely that Galton had come to Paris at the age of seventy only to argue the merits of fingerprints and anthropometry. Bertillon's renown as the inventor of the first system of identification has obscured the fact that he was the most advanced photographer in Europe. Ever since Galton had devised his method of composite photography in collaboration with Herbert Spencer he had kept in touch with developments in photographic technique. As the classic book *Enquiries into Human Faculty* shows, he had used it to try to illustrate how the photographs of human faces, superimposed upon each other, could be used to demonstrate common anthropological characteristics in different individuals. The technique is difficult, and the interpretation of the results uncertain, but at that time Galton seems to have attached considerable importance to it. If there was anyone likely to be able to suggest methods of improving the photographic technique it would have been Bertillon. In any situation of this kind he was at his best. He was a first-class technician and experimental demonstrator. The regard which Galton is known to have had for Bertillon no doubt dates from this occasion, the only one, apparently, on which they ever met.

Although among the most distinguished, Galton was not the first Englishman to show interest in the work of the Department of Judicial Identity and its chief. Among the cards is one of a Dr J. M. Martin, who was Medical Officer of Health to the Stroud District Council in 1883, which was the year when he visited the Prefecture. This was before the Department of Judicial Identity was created and very soon after Bertillon's first success with the new system. Historically it is thus one of the most interesting original documents of them all. It may well be that Dr Martin called at the Prefecture in connexion with some other matter, and upon hearing a report of the new method of identification ultimately reached the young man who had invented it.

For in general, as might be expected, it was not until the '90's that the important visitors and inquirers began to arrive. The Italians preceded Galton. There are the visiting-cards of Garofalo, Ottolenghi, Niceforo, and Ferri, the most distinguished followers of Lombroso, whose theory of the criminal type was making such a furore in Europe just then. They were interested because of the systematized methods of measurement which Bertillon had devised; but they wanted to use them not for the purpose of identifying individuals, but to prove that the criminal type could be recognized by measurements of the head and body. In 1889 the great Lombroso himself had told Ottolenghi that "the Bertillon instruments gave the maximum of precision."

Bertillon was a personal friend of Niceforo, and there is a

SCENE OF A BURGLARY IN 1907, PHOTOGRAPHED BY BERTILLON

The photograph is scaled so as to show the dimensions of the room and the sizes of the objects in it. This is a very fine example of interior photography.

The Unveiling of the Plaque to Bertillon

The ceremony took place on December 17, 1952, at No. 5 Avenue du Président Wilson, the house in which he died.

legend, which may have some truth in it, that at one time he accepted the theory of the criminal type. If he ever did so it was finally abandoned, and the matter is not very important. What is significant is that Lombroso and his colleagues—whatever we may think of their theory—were trained anthropologists devoted to accurate experimental method. They acknowledged that Bertillon's techniques were greatly superior to their own.

There is no evidence that these distinguished men were in any way influenced adversely by the reverberations of the Dreyfus Affair. They were continually in touch with Bertillon in Paris, and Niceforo never failed to visit the Prefecture when he was there. A note is written on one of his cards: " Ma femme et moi nous vous envoyons ainsi qu'à Madame Bertillon nos vœux bien affectueux de bonne année."

Germans also came regularly. The cards of the distinguished Professor of Criminology in the University of Berlin, Schneickert, are there. He was also a caller who did not need to make an appointment. One of his cards is inscribed, " Viendra [?] cet après-midi." He also never failed to visit the Prefecture when in Paris. There is also the card of the internationally known fingerprint expert Heindl. He was then Royal Commissioner of Police in Dresden. Although at an early stage he abandoned anthropometry for fingerprints, he wrote in a foreword to a book as lately as 1938, " Paris became the Mecca of the police, and Bertillon their prophet." This is a statement of historical fact by one of the first authorities upon the history of identification.

Although Scotland Yard never fully adopted the Bertillon system, in 1902 they were closely in touch with the work of his department. The visiting-card of Macnaghten, at that time Chief Constable in the Metropolitan Police, is in the file. He was second-in-command to Henry, the inventor of the fingerprint system which bears his name. Next to his chief, Macnaghten was the greatest authority in Great Britain both on fingerprints and on the Bertillon system. Henry had operated the system in India before it was replaced by fingerprints. Photography may then well have been their chief common interest. Scotland Yard, in common with all other police organizations throughout the world, was indebted to Bertillon for his methods of judicial photography.

The most important of all his visitors arrived almost last of all. In 1913 the Duke of Windsor, then Prince of Wales, visited the department with his friend the Marquis of Breteuil. Embarrassed as he always was by formal visits, and the more so on this occasion, since he had never received Royalty before, Bertillon was soon to find that this was no mere princely gesture. The heir to the throne of England was genuinely interested and even fascinated by the things he was told and shown, and particularly by the classification and method of adapting it to the location of the individual cards. If Bertillon had looked forward to this visit with apprehension it vanished as he warmed to his work of exposition. The Prince of Wales was introduced to the holy of holies. For some time Bertillon had been collecting material for a small criminological museum which was his special pride. Only the most favoured visitors were admitted to it.

It gave the last touch required to make the visit a success. Since he had undertaken the examination of questioned documents as part of the duties of his department, he had acquired an exceptionally good collection of forged postage-stamps, and he had become a considerable authority upon this kind of fraud. He may have known that King George V was an enthusiastic stamp-collector, and a great authority. In any case, it immediately became evident that the Prince shared his father's enthusiasm :

> It was then that I saw his collector's eye brighten, and some days afterwards he put a number of questions to me concerning the manner whereby forged postage-stamps can be recognized. It was a pleasure to me to complete his education, for he already knew a great deal about the subject. [See Appendix IV.]

This is the reason why he laid so much store by the photograph and, perhaps *a fortiori*, by the medal which the great-grandmother of one of his last visitors, and the most distinguished, had given him. The visits of both great and small were not, in fact, to continue much longer. Bertillon had less than two years to live.

II

Friends

Proust's gloomy verdict that after the Dreyfus Affair there were no friendships but political ones was not true in the case of Bertillon. His relationship with Lacassagne, who is said to have disagreed with his findings concerning the *bordereau* at a very early stage, weathered the storm when it broke. His friend, a Lyonese of working-class origin, could be as blunt and direct as any Yorkshireman, but he was a man of the soundest judgment in matters of judicial proof and the validity of opinion evidence. Extremely cautious in such matters himself, he was of opinion that Bertillon's customary caution had forsaken him on this occasion. But he was to find Bertillon, as others did, absolutely unsusceptible to argument in this matter. He was content to express his opinion—it was forcibly done—and afterwards agree to differ. With this understanding between them, there was no interruption of their personal relationship.

This can be explained by the complementary courses which their two careers had taken, and by the fact that their community of interest was rooted in the same kind of social attitude.

When Bertillon was a young man and a cadet member of his father's Society of Anthropology he had first met Jean-Alexandre-Eugène Lacassagne. Lacassagne was ten years older, and he was to become one of the great medico-legists of his day. In the early days of their careers Bertillon and Lacassagne had seen little of each other. The Prefecture clerk was fighting his battles in Paris; Lacassagne was a physician attached to the French army in Africa. He distinguished himself technically there by his study of tattooing; it was an important investigation to which anthropologists owe a great deal. When a Chair of Forensic Medicine was founded at Lyon in 1884 Lacassagne was invited to accept it.

He was to prove much more than a distinguished medico-legist. Lacassagne was among the company of those great men of the nineteenth century who were acutely alive to the social implications of science. Having great erudition and an encyclopædic memory, he had no patience with men who were preoccupied with learning more and more about less and less. On the other hand, he was no blind opponent of specialization. When it was proposed that the Chairs of Forensic Medicine and Forensic Chemistry at Lyon should be combined he insisted upon their separation, because he said that his knowledge of and taste for chemistry did not suffice to justify the combination of medicine and chemistry within the same faculty. At a period when—and not only in France—it was assumed as a matter of course that competence in medicine necessarily included sufficient knowledge of and skill in chemistry this was an unconventional point of view. But Lacassagne had his way. Cazeneuve, a chemist, was appointed to an independent Chair of Toxicology. This was the real beginning of the era of forensic science. Previously the only science and art which had been brought to the problems of criminal investigation were those of medicine. It was the appreciation of this larger context which made Lacassagne so enthusiastic an advocate of Bertillon. Medical science was no longer sufficient to cover the whole forensic field.

For Lacassagne there was a larger context still. Apart from his medico-legal work, which included a comprehensive programme of lecturing not only to medical and legal students but to laymen as well, he played an energetic part in the sociological controversies of his period. He was among the most formidable of Lombroso's opponents, and his words at the Congress of Criminal Anthropology at Rome in 1886 have no less, and perhaps more, significance to-day than they had then. He strongly contested the theory which Lombroso then held that criminals were born and not made :

> The social milieu is also important. Perhaps you will allow me to borrow an analogy from a modern theory. The social milieu is the culture-broth of criminality; the microbe is the criminal, an element which has no importance until it finds the medium upon which it can grow . . . Societies get the criminals they deserve.

Thus perhaps also it was the strong social conscience they

shared which was the strongest bond between the two men. It is often forgotten that scientific methods for the control and detection of crime acquit the innocent as positively and finally as they convict the guilty. Not only the inefficiency of the old Prefecture methods had shocked Bertillon, but also their injustice. It was not for nothing that he called his service the Department of Judicial Identity. His work was a social contribution, because it made justice an integral part of the processes of criminal investigation. The notion that if a dog were given a bad name he could be hanged on the theory that if not guilty as charged he was still in general culpable as an enemy of society was hateful to Bertillon. The genius of the man made him in a larger sense an enemy of society himself, so that he knew what it felt like—" *un mauvais caractère inimaginable.*"

It was therefore inevitable that Bertillon should bring his prestige and influence to bear upon the development of the new era of forensic science of which Lacassagne was also a pioneer. The professor met almost as much resistance when he founded the Laboratory of Technical Police at Lyon as had Bertillon in the matter of anthropometry. Officials of the Prefecture were sceptical and obstructive. They would grant no funds to finance the new department, and for many years the now famous laboratory subsisted precariously from hand to mouth upon such fees as it could secure from private work.

Nothing can deprive Bertillon of the merit of having not only initiated the first method of identification, but of having thereby established principles which were to be applied in a much wider field. He was to live to see methods evolved for the identification of blood-groups, the classification of forensic dusts and minute debris found on the scene of the crime, and the identification of hairs and fibres by methods essentially based upon the principles he had laid down. It was this common inspiration of Lacassagne and Bertillon and of scores of others which could not be dislocated by a disagreement concerning the merits of the Dreyfus case.

The controversy never came between Bertillon and his old students:

DEAR BERTILLON,

I give you all my thanks for the way you have received me, and all that you have done for me; and I remain your servant and pupil.

PIERRO LOMAÑA

This was a note, dated 1909, written by a young Spanish professor in the University of Barcelona who had been his pupil. To quote a more renowned example, it had no influence upon the devoted Reiss. The abundance of his visiting-cards testifies to the frequency with which he came to see his old chief. Some details of his history reveal the profound influence which Bertillon's teaching and personality had upon him. By birth a German-Jew, he had studied at Lausanne and had become a Swiss subject. Interested in the Bertillon system, he had remained to study it for two years.

Reiss was a man of choleric habit. During his student days it was severely tried by a strange misadventure. He suffered from an affection of the heart which sometimes resulted in coma. During one particularly grave attack, doctors pronounced his life to be extinct. Since he was by religion a Catholic, the supposed corpse was prepared for burial by being placed in an open coffin surrounded by candles in a chapel of repose, as the local custom was. Many friends visited the chapel to pay their last respects. In the middle of these proceedings Reiss returned to consciousness, and sat up in his coffin. It appears that he had immediately regained full possession of his faculties. Taking in the scene, and concluding, not unnaturally, that he was the victim of some elaborate practical joke, his characteristic choler took possession of him. Reiss addressed his congregation in language very inappropriate to the place and the occasion. It was an embarrassing and even terrifying moment. The spectators are said to have taken to their heels, leaving the future director of the Institute of Scientific Police struggling with his shroud.

If the coma had ended as the doctors thought that in fact it had, Bertillon would never have trained one of his most distinguished pupils. Without distinction as a theoretician, Reiss was a brilliant and conscientious technician. His textbook of judicial photography is still a classic. The cold ferocity which Bertillon knew so well how to assume could overawe even a man of Reiss's temperament. So devoted was the man to his master and his work that he never forgot it, even in his leisure-time. The circumstances made no difference. Invited to dine at the house of a distinguished hostess, he was not at ease until he had succeeded in diverting the conversation into channels of a discussion concerning the ideal uniform for Parisian police officers. He was not invited again. But it is a tribute to the kind of enthusiasm which Bertillon could inspire that Reiss returned to Lausanne to found, with the support of a large part of his own fortune, the Institute of Scientific Police there in 1902.

Of all his students his most distinguished one, Dr Edmond Locard, was his devoted friend, and understood him, so far as anyone could understand Alphonse Bertillon. Far from being blind to his faults, he has said of him that it was his invincible integrity which inspired his friends and disconcerted his enemies. The rudeness of which his critics complained, and which they thought studied, stemmed, in fact, from his dislike of finesse, which he thought hypocritical. His confidence once gained, he was a loyal and constant friend. When Dr Locard became director of the laboratory at Lyon, Bertillon never lost touch with its progress. He followed with great interest the work on fingerprints, and in particular Locard's technique of poroscopy, the identification of the sweat pores which lie along the ridges of every fingerprint. Locard proved that the pores vary in number, size, and position in every individual. Bertillon's interest in this research is further evidence—if any is required—of the breadth of his outlook where any problem of identification was concerned.

Although the Dreyfus Affair produced a breach, it could not destroy the strong community of interests and tastes within the Bertillon family. It was his father and grandfather who had first introduced him to the delights of anthropology. Alphonse Bertillon repaid this in kind by the support and co-operation which he gave to his brother Jacques, who had succeeded his father as a statistician at the Hôtel de Ville. The statistical data which each was collecting were of value to the other. Georges, the younger brother, owed his doctoral thesis to Alphonse. He had always said while a student that here was material ready-made for an academic dissertation. Not only his thesis but his statistical work thereafter was linked to his brother's inspiration. Even if divided on the affective plane, they held together as a scientific team.

For, despite the controversy which had involved them as a family, Dr Jacques Bertillon when he went to the United States on a visit was proud to find his brother's name upon every one's lips. Even the Negro porters, on seeing the name *Bertillon* on his luggage, wanted to know if he were related to the " fingerprint man." And it is a matter of history that Bertillon's reputation stood higher in America than in any other country in the world. It had not sensibly diminished on account of the Dreyfus case.

If Alphonse Bertillon was flattered when his brother brought him this news on his return he did not show it.

" I know about that," he said. " I have heard from an American publisher. He wants me to write my memoirs—a dollar a word. What do you think of that? "

" You are not going to do it, Alphonse? "

" No, I have refused. After all, I am Chief of the Service of Judicial Identity. It wouldn't be suitable. But he also said that perhaps I might prefer to write some detective stories at the same figure. Now, that is an idea."

" What! " said his horrified brother. " What! I didn't know you were in the least interested in such things."

" I love detective stories. Calm yourself, my dear fellow— Pascal is still my favourite author. But this Conan Doyle is a most remarkable man. I should like to meet him. His Sherlock Holmes sometimes confuses certainty with presumption, but there is analytical genius there, and what a vision of the future of the scientific police! Yes, when I retire I shall write detective stories."

His brother caught the blue glint of ferocious sarcasm in the Bertillon eye. He laughed.

" Very well, Alphonse. You will write detective stories— when you retire."

" Long hence," said Alphonse Bertillon.

But it was not to be so long.

23. " LEBEN IST DOCH SO SÜSS "

BERTILLON'S indifferent health had always exasperated him and certainly contributed to the asperities of his temperament. The migraine from which he had suffered as a boy never left him. His digestive system functioned badly, so that he could neither drink nor smoke without ill-effects. During his later years he was obliged to conform to a strict diet.

These disabilities contributed to an unsociability which was not fundamentally a part of his nature. He could enjoy company, make his contribution in it, and expand in a favourable social climate. It has been said of him that the misfortune of the Dreyfus Affair aggravated his natural misanthropy and wish to escape his fellow-men. It is more probable that his deteriorating health, which he ignored as far as he could, made him abandon social commitments.

For he would not abandon his work, and there was not sufficient physical energy for both work and society. He had voluntarily lived in exacting harness, and he died in that harness. It was in keeping that he should do so. Bertillon was not of the stuff of which good invalids are made.

There is a photograph of him taken in his fifty-eighth or fifty-ninth year wherefrom it is clear that the shadow of death was upon him. The structure of the face, always fine-drawn, is dangerously hollowed, and the eyes have receded far into the head. His family, and particularly his wife, saw the natural pallor of his complexion intensified.

They were in great anxiety, which was the more acute because it was not admitted openly. Bertillon's sensitive pride and extreme reticence did not encourage any discussion of the condition of his health. This was a matter for medical men. Having a great respect for the faculty, he followed instructions to the letter and lived his life according to the régime his doctors formulated. This was the only concession he thought it necessary to make to the frailties of the body.

But he knew that he was soon to make the last journey, however loath he was even to hint of such a thing to others. Eastward of the Boulevard Ménilmontant, in the 20th Arrondissement, is the Cemetery of the East, called Père-Lachaise. He had a mind to visit it—one wintry Sunday morning of all times, when snow lay thick upon the ground. Three of them joined him on this strange excursion—Jacques, Georges, and Amélie, his wife, who insisted upon accompanying them. On the journey and during the subsequent walk they were treated to one of the famous Bertillon silences; and the rest took their cue from him and kept their own counsel.

The place was silent to a degree that only deep snow can give, and absolutely deserted. The stones and monuments of a burial ground where Mussulmen, Jews, and Christians rest had lost their contours under the heavy white layer. Suddenly Alphonse Bertillon broke the silence. He stood still, looking down on the snow.

" It is here that I want to be buried."

This sudden remark was made with no emphasis, and was addressed to no one in particular, but he turned towards his wife. He seemed greatly disturbed when she suddenly burst into tears. To turn it off he said:

" Do not worry, Amélie. After all, I am still living."

She remained in tears, but through them spoke in German.

" *Leben ist doch so süss!* I was thinking of my own death. If you must be buried here I won't leave you. It gives me a shock to think of it standing here. I am afraid of death—yes, I am afraid of it!"

This incident perhaps explains how it came about that Amélie Bertillon outlived her husband eighteen years (she died in 1932) in absolute retreat from reality. Fearing life without him as much as death itself, it seems inevitable that she should develop fantasies of persecution. However difficult life must sometimes have been with him (and it must have been very difficult indeed), without him it was insupportable.

It was not long after this that a serious deterioration in his health set in. Life with him both at home and in his office became more difficult, since he became abnormally sensitive to cold. The room in which he lived or worked required to be heated to a very high temperature, because he was otherwise attacked with fits of shivering by reason of a chronically sub-normal temperature. His sight, so necessary to the efficient performance of his work, was impaired.

At the earnest request of his doctors, there was a specialist conference : the diagnosis—pernicious anæmia. Had this occurred in our own time it is probable that Bertillon's life would have been saved. At that time it was the equivalent of a sentence of death.

There was in 1913 only one remedy, and even this was regarded as revolutionary and not to be applied except in the last resort. This was blood transfusion. At a period when much less was known concerning blood-groupings than has been discovered to-day it was a dangerous operation and the results were uncertain.

His brother Georges gave his blood. At that time the method was direct transference of the blood of the donor from artery to vein—a difficult and uncertain process, since an incision into the artery was necessary and the quantity of blood taken could not be even approximately controlled. The operators overdid it. Dr Georges Bertillon had a syncope.

The results of the transfusion were temporarily very promis-ing. Those who witnessed it were astounded at the sudden change for the better which the treatment produced. The subnormal temperature rose; the extreme lassitude dis-appeared. But the respite was only temporary. Within some three months the anæmic symptoms had returned as vigorously as ever. Another transfusion was attempted, and then a third, with results which were progressively less satisfactory.

If blood transfusions could have saved him he would have lived. In spite of the ill-effects of the first experience, it was brother Georges who offered himself each time as the donor. Bertillon had a faculty for making himself disliked, and many who respected him found his tongue and his temper too much ever to risk any friendly advance; but the fundamental quality of his affection is better shown in the solid loyalty of his friends and family.

He continued to attend his office as long as he could. There, also, he was understood. It was not only that every one recognized his ability and achievements. Although severe, he never lost the habit of treating his subordinates with consideration, his more inexcusable behaviour being reserved for people of his own calibre. Those who worked with him fully shared the anxiety of his family and closest friends, although no one was bold enough to show it. Indiscretions of this kind provoked immediate and unpleasant reactions.

The reason for this perhaps was that, like his wife, Bertillon still found life sweet. In spite of a temperament which had made him his own worst enemy, a wilfully neglected early education, and a life-long bad health, so long as there was anything to achieve life was worth living.

He had to retire more and more often to his chaise-longue, and into the long silences which were habitual to him, but now lengthened of necessity. But at intervals he still talked with restrained enthusiasm of the past, perhaps remembering the chaise-longue of his boyhood's days to which he had retired the more energetically to defy his family. Had it not been for this invalidism much would have been lost to us concerning his private life, but he talked during his last days particularly to his niece Suzanne. He was a near neighbour of his brother Jacques, her father, who lived in the Avenue Marceau. He had no children, and his nieces were often with him.

The man who, although contemptuous of sympathy, never failed to let all the world know if his little finger ached reacted quite differently under the shadow of death. His niece has made a 'speaking likeness' of him very different from the anthropometric pictures to which he was devoted. He no longer lectured and laid down the law, which he liked to do when *en famille*. What interested him was the history of the Bertillon clan, and the manner whereby his life-work was linked with that of his father and grandfather. This in itself was something foreign to his earlier style. It has been complained of Bertillon with a good deal of justice that he never made adequate acknowledgment of his debt to the work of others, but he repaid that debt in full in those last days when he confided in his niece and told her of the guerrilla warfare at school, the fruitful days at Montmorency and Ussat, and of how the work of father and grandfather had inspired him to embark upon his great experiment of the measurement of the criminal anatomy. Had not the known approach of death softened and broken down his characteristic reserve no adequate biography of Bertillon could have been written. It has been possible to show that the man was something much larger than the work he did—significant though it is—precisely because of the ' confessions' made to his niece in the last few months that he had to live.

For the rest, the thing that preoccupied him was the future of the beloved motherland. Bertillon shared the anxiety of the biologists and anthropologists of his day concerning the biological future of France. The statistical work of his father and brother and their colleagues on the subject of the national fertility made depressing reading, and it was a fashionable theory among the specialists in the vital sciences that France was in decline, and that the Germanic race would become supreme in Europe. The German menace obsessed him, as it did so many Frenchmen of his day, and he prophesied that in the near future France would be fighting for her life. He did not live to see the black days of August 1914.

It was this fervid, if critical, patriotism which had partly determined his dangerously subjective approach to the Dreyfus matter. One of the reasons why Bertillon became involved in an affair which was to take so tragic a turn both for victim and executioner was that he conceived it as his duty to France to investigate the problem. In common with many other honourable and upright men he saw the *bordereau* as one of the symptoms of a vast conspiracy to defeat and destroy France. He never altered his opinion to the day of his death. Only a month before his passing he was to reaffirm it with all the old intransigence.

He had received the red ribbon in 1893, but the Rosette had never been offered to him—as some said, because he was on the wrong side in the Dreyfus Affair. At the beginning of 1914—he was then very ill—he was recommended for the

Officer's Rosette of the Légion d'Honneur. It is a measure of the force of the passion and prejudice the Dreyfus trials had stirred up that even fifteen years later his part in the affair remained fresh in the official mind, with the strange result that a representative of the Minister was entrusted with the delicate task of interviewing Bertillon and explaining to him under what conditions the Rosette could be offered to him. They were that he should retract what he had affirmed on the subject of the *bordereau*.

Whoever formulated this gambit was singularly ignorant of Bertillon's character. The emissary must have been an acutely unhappy man as he stumbled through his diplomatic formulæ concerning the great services to the Republic which the Minister was the first to recognize, but in the matter of the Dreyfus *bordereau* policy compelled him to inquire about M. Bertillon's present view concerning that matter, and if it were changed in any way.

The dying man, lying on his chaise-longue, had listened in silence to the oration. He suddenly sat up. There was a glint in his eyes, charged with all the old ferocity.

" No !" he said violently. " No !"

This was but a short time before he became blind. It was the final signal that there could be no more work and that there was nothing left for him to do. The uncontrolled despair of his wife worried him. Amélie nursed him devotedly, but between times used to wander from room to room praying that she might die if his life could be spared. Her reaction also worried and embarrassed his family, who shared her distress and anxiety. It was not their way to meet a crisis with lamentations and the wringing of hands. No one yet realized that the balance of Amélie Bertillon's reason was already disturbed.

It was late in the evening of February 13 that the awaited crisis occurred. Alphonse Bertillon sank into a light coma. The breathing shallowed almost to vanishing point. Once or twice he opened his eyes and tried to speak what is believed to have been his wife's name. He died at 11 o'clock.

His brother Jacques returned to Number 26 to tell his wife and daughter the news. He was composed, but they saw that he was trembling slightly.

" He is dead."

Apart from the rest, Amélie Bertillon was noisily weeping. Three days later, on February 16, Bertillon was buried with national honours. At his own wish he lies in a vault in Père-Lachaise where his younger brother, Georges, joined him in 1919. He would have been horribly embarrassed had he been there to see the great crowd that came to pay their last respects to him at the graveside, but it was a greater tribute to his memory than the dreadful *pompe funèbre* of the official obsequies. It is a remarkable fact that a man so remote and unapproachable, and one with an almost pathological dread of publicity, should, in spite of it all, somehow have become not only recognized, as he fully deserved, as a man of science but popularly admired as a person. This is the enduring memorial to him, and the one which he would most have appreciated himself.

On the south-east side of the 15th Arrondissement there is a short street which connects the Rue de Vouillé with the Rue de la Procession north of it. It is called Rue Alphonse Bertillon. There are some who think that it is a too remote and insignificant memorial to him, but on the other hand he is commemorated in distinguished company. Less than a kilo-metre north are the Boulevards Garibaldi and Pasteur. It is perhaps less appropriate that in the same area Emile Zola has his avenue and even his Métro station.

24. THE AFFAIR OF THE GRAND DUCHESS

MORE than seventy years have passed since the young Prefecture clerk sat at his desk cutting up photographs of the human face and pasting them side by side on pieces of cardboard. This operation, which his colleagues thought so eccentric, and which so much irritated his first chief, was in fact as significant as any of his early experiments. In some respects it is the most significant of all. Bertillon's anthropometry is a period piece. It no longer has any practical importance in the technique of identification. Strictly, it was superseded as early as 1892 when Galton published his proof of the uniqueness of fingerprints.

This is not true of his great work in the field of judicial photography and of what is called the *portrait parlé*. His anthropological pictures (so to call them) are not an infallible means of identification as his anthropometric measurements or as fingerprints are; but they have uses which are quite as valuable to-day as they were in his own time.

His sectional photographs were designed to solve the problem of recognition as distinct from formal and exact identification. Mistaken identity always remains a serious matter in any judicial inquiry. As every one knows, it can lead to grave miscarriages of justice. Bertillon's method of accurate photography and a detailed study of its results was designed to overcome this difficulty. The case of Rollin (page 103) is a striking example of the success of his principles and method.

What is more significant is that this part of his work has not only survived him, but is, in some respects, still indispensable for the solution of certain problems of identification.

Alphonse Bertillon was a year old when Roger Tichborne was drowned at sea in April 1854. He was in his fourteenth year when the singular meeting took place in Paris between the bemused Lady Tichborne and the obese and grotesque creature who claimed to be her long-lost son. She gave it in evidence at the trial that on January 11, 1867, she had seen him at the Hôtel de Lille et d'Albion lying on his bed in his clothes. Convinced of his identity, she had kissed him, saying that he looked like his father and his ears looked like his uncle's.

The trial at which the claimant was non-suited began in 1871 and lasted 118 days. A criminal prosecution which followed dragged on for 188 days. Bertillon was at this time preparing to struggle with his belated *baccalauréat*. Had this affair occurred ten years later his *portrait parlé* might conceivably have saved the Tichborne estate a very large sum of money. This, one of the longest processes in English legal history, might never have been begun but for the obstinate wishful thinking of Lady Tichborne; but, having begun, it bade fair to continue indefinitely. At long last it came to an end, and the imposter was convicted; but it was also said by Griffiths, the Deputy Governor of Millbank, whither the prisoner was committed, that even some of his warders believed that the man was innocent of any crime.

Physical evidence of identity was given to rebut Lady Tichborne's obsessional conviction that Arthur Orton, the impersonator of Roger Tichborne, was indeed her son, because, *inter alia*, " his ears looked like his uncle's "; but evidently it was not universally accepted. Had this evidence been thought final it would have been the end of the matter. But, in the event, the trial of the claimant continued for six months, and this when he had been deprived by death of his most vital witness, the lady who claimed that she was his mother.

The physical evidence was that photographs and portraits of Roger Tichborne were compared with those of the claimant, but not in the systematized fashion whereby Bertillon made his investigations when he developed his *portrait parlé*. Whether the material would have been sufficient for him to have arrived at a definite conclusion is of course uncertain, but it was precisely the kind of case with which his system was designed to deal.

Bertillon was too young to play any part in the Tichborne affair, and was never fortunate enough to be associated with any case of fraud by impersonation on this scale. The anthropometry in the sense of body measurement did not survive his death, and it had, in fact, been abandoned altogether by most countries. This adapted use of the *portrait parlé* was to be vindicated fourteen years after his death in a case in many respects as remarkable as the Tichborne affair.

On February 7, 1928, the *Berengaria* arrived in New York. There was one woman passenger who had scarcely left her cabin during the voyage, but it was rumoured that she was yet another highly placed refugee from the Russian Revolution, and none other than the Grand Duchess Anastasie Nikolaiévna, the youngest daughter of the Czar, and the only survivor of the murdered royal family who died at Ekaterinburg, in Siberia, in July 1918.

Owing to fog, the *Berengaria* did not arrive in harbour until February 9. The daughter of the Czar refused to answer questions, but it was reported that her identity was vouched for by Prince Constantine Gabriel, head of the Russian refugees in Berlin, and by a Mr Gleb Botkin, a son of the physician of the Imperial family. She had arrived at New York as the guest of Mrs William B. Leeds, who had formerly been Princess Xenia.

As in the case of the Tichborne pretender, there is no doubt that Madame Tchaikovsky, as she now called herself, had a number of distinguished supporters who believed her to be the Grand Duchess. Her story was consistent enough and did not vary. She had contrived to escape with the help of a Russian soldier, named Tchaikovsky. They had reached Bucharest, where they had married. She had emeralds sewn up in her clothing on the sale of which they lived. In 1920 she had come to Berlin.

In his action to secure the Tichborne estates Arthur Orton had been able to call eight-five witnesses, who included Lady Tichborne herself, the family solicitor, six magistrates, and a number of distinguished army men who gave positive evidence in good faith that his claim was true. Madame Tchaikovsky was not able to summon such a formidable array, but she had considerable support among the refugee circle in Berlin. She was by no means the only claimant at that time for Russian Imperial honours, but she seems to have been more successful than any other in gaining adherents. Considerable sympathy was felt for her in some quarters. She had said, and it may have been true, that her husband had been killed by Russian agents in Bucharest. In February 1920 she had tried to drown herself in the Spree. Being rescued, she was sent to an asylum. Madame Tchaikovsky gained rather than lost support on account of this attempt at suicide. After such ordeals many thought it not surprising that her mind should have been affected.

She had been 'identified' by Gleb Botkin, who declared that he had known her at the age of seven, when he himself was eight years old. The evidence which seems most to have impressed her supporters was that of an old nurse of the Imperial family brought to Berlin to identify her. Her name was Sascha, and there was no doubt as to her bona fides. Not only did she identify her as the Grand Duchess, but Madame Tchaikovsky when they met immediately addressed her by her pet name of Zhura.

On the other hand, a large and influential section of the Russian community, which included the Grand Dukes Boris and Cyril, repudiated her claims. Captain Djamgaroff believed her insane: " It has not been definitely proved who she really is, although there is no doubt she is insane, suffering from a mania of persecution with its usual symptom, the mania of grandeur."

In spite of this powerful opposition Madame Tchaikovsky maintained her ambiguous position for seven years. There was no conclusive evidence to show that her claim was false.

At the beginning of 1927 matters came to a head. Frau von Ratieff had published her memoirs, wherein she had defended Madame Tchaikovsky's claims and had accused one of the Grand Dukes of a conspiracy to discredit her, because her claim endangered his inheritance of certain funds and property. It was as a result of this crisis that a technical investigation of this curious problem began.

On January 25, 1927, Professor Gilliard, of Lausanne, requested Professor Mark Bischoff to make an examination of a number of photographs of the Grand Duchess Anastasie,

and to compare them with photographs of Madame Tchaikovsky and if possible to report whether or not they were photographs of one and the same person.

Professor Bischoff, of the Institute of Scientific Police of
Lausanne, had succeeded Dr Reiss, Bertillon's pupil, as
Director. His report upon these photographs was one in which
Bertillon himself would have rejoiced. For this examination Professor Bischoff made use of Bertillon's technique
("signalement descriptif, méthode Alphonse Bertillon connue
sous le nom de 'Portrait parlé'").

The profile portraits and the ears were rephotographed and
scaled to exactly the same proportional size. In the case of the
features the points of reference were the length of the face
from the eyebrows to the bottom of the chin. In the case of
the ear the total length was used as reference. The profiles
were twice partially superimposed in a manner used for stamp-
ing two heads upon certain coins. In the first the head of the
Duchess Anastasie is uppermost; in the second the order is
reversed. These photographs demonstrate in a striking manner
the marked differences of the two profiles, and particularly in
the form of the nose.

It was believed by the Italian anthropologists of the School
of Lombroso that the convolutions of the ear were unique for
the individual. Bertillon was also of this opinion, although this
uniqueness cannot be experimentally demonstrated as in the
case of fingerprints. However this may be, it was the form
and convolutional pattern of the ears which proved beyond all
doubt that the Grand Duchess and Madame Tchaikovsky
were not the same person. Two photographs of the Grand
Duchess, taken in 1912 and before her death in 1918, show a
right ear of the same form. It has a narrow border and a large
area at the top almost without convolutions. Madame
Tchaikovsky's ear, on the other hand, differs not only in
general form, but the border is more pronounced and the convolutions involve a much larger area. In their fashion these
ears are as unlike as two fingerprints with the designs of an
arch and a whorl.

Begun in February, the work was not completed until
October, because further comparisons were made between the

photographs of other daughters of the Imperial family and those of Madame Tchaikovsky whereby it was shown that the facial characteristics of the claimant were also quite inconsistent with those of the other daughters of the Czar.

This was not the conclusion of a remarkable investigation. Perhaps on account of these reports, Madame Tchaikovsky sailed for New York early in 1928. Several of the American papers published a photograph purporting to be one of the claimant. The comparison of this photograph with that of the Grand Duchess was made the subject of a further report by Professor Bischoff on June 23, 1928. As in the previous examination, the photograph of the Grand Duchess (in this case one taken in 1913) was rephotographed to a scale to correspond exactly to the dimensions of the questioned one. On comparing the details, it was obvious that Professor Bischoff's conclusion was justified. The photographs agreed in every essential respect :

> From this evidence, the alleged portrait of Madame Tchaikovsky appearing in *The New York Evening Post* of February 7, 1928, is a retouched reproduction of the photograph of the Grand Duchess Anastasie Nikolaiévna.

This success was all the more remarkable because the examiners could not choose their standards of comparison and were obliged to work upon the material available. The young Grand Duchess had then been dead for more than eight years. No accurate photographs in the judicial sense of the term had ever been taken of her. It is fortunate that at least two became available which showed features having a high value for the purposes of identification. The most valuable piece of identifying evidence was the two photographs of the right ear, taken at an interval of six years, and showing no fundamental structural change.

This case is a particularly striking example of the solution of a problem of identification which arises over and over again in the civil and criminal courts of all countries. It is not, of course, always possible to solve a problem of identification by reference to a photograph which was not originally taken under controlled conditions; but in cases where no other evidence of identification exists or where the evidence is doubtful an investigation—of which the Tchaikovsky case is now a classic example—has to be made. If conclusive proof is possible the finding of the facts will depend upon the application of the principle and practice which Bertillon first formulated more than seventy years ago.

25. CONCLUSION

ON March 15, 1914, a month after the death of Alphonse Bertillon, Professor Lacassagne and Dr Locard wrote memorial papers in the *Archives of Criminal Anthropology and Legal Medicine* (No. 243).

These papers are both of great interest. The first emphasizes Bertillon's qualities as a man; the second, his achievements as scientist and technologist.

Professor Lacassagne's concluding words were that Bertillon was a man above the common sort who had nothing of which to complain because he had attacked with great resolution a difficult task, and that he had lived to realize in his maturity a dream of his youth. [. . . cet homme supérieur. Bertillon n'est pas à plaindre, il a fait avec entêtement une longue tâche : sa vie a été suffisante pour réaliser dans l'âge mûr une pensée de sa jeunesse."]

This sums up as sharply as any one sentence could the full achievement of the man. It is hoped that this study of his life has made it clear that from the very first he was dedicated to some such task as the one he so brilliantly completed. To his worried and often exasperated family it must at times have seemed impossible that the barbarous Alphonse could make a success of his life at all, much less that he would make one of the great discoveries of the century, and that he would extract from it its maximum social and technical use. It is not difficult to imagine not only the great satisfaction but the extreme surprise with which Bertillon's distinguished father read the report his son had addressed to the Prefect of Police. As has been seen, Dr Bertillon, despite his affection for the black sheep of the family, had written him off as a total loss in any sense that he understood success. It was the last reward of a man who had done his best in a difficult situation to die fully realizing the great significance of the discovery his son had made.

For Bertillon's anthropometry would have much less significance if it were merely a police matter. In the circumstances it is most fortunate that he should have become a clerk in the Prefecture of Police, because it was precisely there that the problem of the identification of the person was the most urgent and immediate. For this reason Bertillon had facilities for the development of his work which might have been lacking had he made the discovery in other circumstances. But the principles of his anthropometry had, and still have, applications unrelated to the criminal field. The importance, for example, of the identification of Rollin is not concerned with crime. No real crime had been committed. The true significance of the process is that a member of the community presumed to be dead was proved, after all, to be alive. Again, it was not sentiment alone which required that those lost in the disaster of the *Drummond Castle* should, if possible, be positively identified. In this case, it is not known to what extent Bertillon's investigation helped to solve the problem of identity, but the British Government thought his work sufficiently important to decorate him.

His life-long friend, Niceforo, in his book *La Police et l'Enquête Judiciaire Scientifiques*, draws attention to the value of anthropometry and the *portrait parlé* in quite a different field—that of historical research. He speaks of its use in the identification of unknown or doubtful busts when there exists a known standard of comparison, and he also gives an interesting account of the examination by Bertillon's methods of the four busts of Nero in the Louvre. Three of them agree closely. They depict a man with a small forehead, rather prominent brows, a small chin, and somewhat protruding eyes. The measurements and photographs of the fourth bust show an exaggeration of all the faults. The forehead is smaller, the brow more protruding, the chin is very small. It was concluded that the three busts in which the facial measurements agree are the realistic portrait of Nero. The fourth was executed later under the growing influence of the tradition of Nero as tyrant and incendiary.

Niceforo also applied the same technique to the study of anthropological characteristics persisting in great families, and to the study of ancient racial types, particularly the Assyrians and Egyptians.

Bertillon was not the discoverer of the principles or even the practice of anthropometry. Manouvrier, Broca, Ottolenghi, and his own father and grandfather are representative examples of the distinguished men who created this branch of applied science. Bertillon's achievement was to devise the technical means whereby measurements of the head and body could be standardized and given the maximum of precision. It is no depreciation of his genius to say that he was, first and foremost, a technologist.

It is this aspect of his great work which is stressed by Dr Edmond Locard, who already in 1914 was successor to Lacassagne as Director of the Laboratory of Police (as it was then called) at Lyon. He says of him that he was a genius because a creator of a new technique which put the police in the way of applied science. [" Il fut un génie, puisqu'il fut un créateur; c'est lui qui créant de toutes pièces une technique nouvelle, fit entrer la police dans la voie des applications scientifiques."] Even more significantly he adds that it was because of his powerful inspiration that an assembly of knowledge and skills has been made which has been given the name of *scientific police*, a pretentiously inexact title which Bertillon did not like, and for which can be substituted police technology [" *technique policière* "].

For, as a technologist, Bertillon was second to none in France, and he probably had no equal in Europe at that time. His report upon the *bordereau* and the evidence he gave make depressing reading, but it is impossible to ignore the conscientious skill and the meticulous accuracy wherewith the report is illustrated. The photomicrographs are excellent. Every measurement made of the handwriting is recorded on the illustrations themselves. The most striking reproduction of all is that of the writing he produced himself in court at Rennes whereby he demonstrated the method by which he considered the *bordereau* had been produced. It is a fortunate thing that he was on the right side of the law. Bertillon would have made a dangerous forger. The writing bears a striking resemblance to that of the document in question.

It is in the anthropometric field that his skill as a technician had the greatest scope. Locard has said that his anthropometric classification is a marvel of mathematical elegance, but it is, in fact, an arithmetical rather than a mathematical feat. This in no way detracts from its merits. But, when all is said, it is the development of the measurement techniques which are uniquely his. Bertillon said to Lacassagne, as he had said to many others, that anyone who was not an imbecile could learn to measure in five minutes and never forget the process. This was his nearest approach to an advertisement of the merits of his own discovery. He meant that he had devised a technique easily workable in practice and applicable to all cases. The experimental evidence amply confirms this. It is no small matter to emphasize that there is no recorded case of mistaken identity through any defect of the anthropometric data.

But the two distinguished men who wrote this *in memoriam* stress, each in his own way, the ultimate fact that the real foundation upon which the work of Alphonse Bertillon was built was a moral and social one. To Lacassagne, a fervid local patriot, it was his Lyonese origin to which he owed the energy, tenacity, and fertile imagination which he brought to everything that he did. Locard, also his life-long friend, who understood him better, has said that his love of precision, even for its own sake, which was almost obsessional, was rooted in the honesty and integrity of his character. It persistently drove him on in the pursuit of truth.

This is, in fact, the legacy he had to bestow not only upon France but upon the rest of the world. In the eighteenth century and for a large part of the nineteenth methods of criminal investigation were corrupt and inefficient. The manner whereby the French police organization was controlled by the spy, the *agent provocateur*, and the confidential *dossier* is well illustrated by the anecdote told by Andrieux—who found Bertillon such a thorn in his side—in his memoirs published after his retirement from the Prefecture. When he was first appointed Prefect his chief clerk came at once to confer with him. The subordinate's first act was to put a *dossier* into his hand, saying that it was the normal practice to hand these papers to the new chief. It was, of course, his own, and it bore the number 14,207. " I have it now in my library," he said, " bound, with all the gross calumnies and truculent denunciations that form the basis of such documents."

Whatever the causes, it is undeniable that great changes for the better took place in police administration and practice towards the end of the nineteenth century. It is no coincidence that these developed side by side with more efficient and highly organized methods of criminal investigation in England, France, and indeed in most European countries. It was not only an organizational but an ethical change. In this respect the Bertillon discoveries were an historical event of the first magnitude. His anthropometry met a social as well as a technical need, and it thus gave a new form and shape to judicial processes and events. It may well be this which explains, on the one hand, the great volume of caricatures in the newspapers—which, had he been aware of this, he ought not to have resented—and, on the other, the Parisian crowds who came to see him laid to rest in Père-Lachaise.

These things are the proper monuments to a man who has left indelible marks of his identity upon the scientific thought and action of his period. They are more significant, if less obtrusive, than the stone and bronze monstrosity beneath which lie his bones. As far as a material monument is concerned, unpolished granite would be more in accord with his style, or, better, the undressed rock which marks the graves of many Yorkshiremen in Wharfedale. In fact, he needs no other memorial than that which he began and finished himself as youth, adolescent, and adult. It is a monument more enduring than brass.

APPENDIX I

Collegiate School, Smethwick

June 17, 1874

Monsieur Bertillon has been with me this last half year as Professor of French. During part of the time he has taken a class in Mathematics.

I have pleasure in stating that he has discharged his duties satisfactorily, and that his character has been unexceptionable.

He leaves me because I have not a sufficient number of pupils to keep him employed.

WILLIAM GRANT, A.C.P.,
Principal

Collegiate School, Bishops Stortford

This is to certify that Monsieur Bertillon, B.A., B.Sc. (Paris)[1] was a master in my school during the third term of the year 1874.

He taught French and occasionally Latin.

He is gentlemanly in appearance and manners, and I believe his morals also are good.

GEO. WILKS, M.A.

Jan. 2, 1875

[1] Mr Wilks appears to have been under the impression that *Bachelier ès lettres* and *Bachelier ès Sciences* were the equivalents of the university titles of Bachelor of Arts and Bachelor of Science in this country.

APPENDIX II

THE ANTHROPOMETRIC CLASSIFICATION

J'ai dit déjà, à propos du portrait parlé, que Bertillon emploie constamment et d'une façon systématique la division tripartite. C'est ce qu'il a fait pour la classification anthropométrique des fiches.

La masse des fiches d'un service sera donc, dans sa méthode, divisée en trois groupes, selon les grandes longueurs de tête, un second les moyennes, un troisième les petites. Puis les grandes longueurs seront divisées en trois sous-groupes selon le largeur de tête. Puis chaque sous-groupe se répartira à son tour en trois classes par les longueurs de médius. Et chaque classe de médius en trois catégories par les longueurs d'auriculaire. Cette division tripartite répétée quatre fois donne $3 \times 3 \times 3 \times 3 = 81$ tiroirs. On peut aller plus loin, en employant par exemple le bizygomatique, ou en faisant intervenir des éléments étrangers à l'anthropométrie comme le numéro de classe de l'iris, ou comme une empreinte digitale systématisée en lettre. En outre, chaque tiroir se subdivise intérieurement par la longueur de pied et par la taille. On voit que les mesures les plus fixes viennent les premières, et les plus approximatives à la fin, comme de juste.

(Edmond Locard, *Traité de Criminalistique*, Tome IV: " Les Preuves de l'Identité," page 622.)

This makes clear the difference between the anthropometric and fingerprint classification. With fingerprints, the primary classification is absolutely determined by two variants, a loop with the arch approximated and the whorl with the composite (now called *compound*) approximated on five pairs of fingers—that is to say, 4^5, equalling 1024 divisions. Anthropometry has no primary classification of this kind, and in fact no fixed primary classification at all. It may rest upon four measurements making 81 divisions as above, or upon five measurements making 243 divisions, which was Henry's arrangement. Theoretically there is no reason why further measurements should not be added. It makes no difference to the principle of threefold division, and in practice simply increases the number of divisions as 3^n.

This should make it clear that there is no difference in principle, and very little in practice, between Henry's 243 anthropometric divisions (Part Three, Chapter 20) and that described in Part Three, Chapter 12.

APPENDIX III

Paris le 24 Octobre 1902

Rapport

Le 17 du courant, j'ai été chargé par M. Jolliot, juge d'instruction, de photographier l'appartement situé au numéro 157 de la rue du Faubourg St-Honoré où un crime avait été commis sur la personne d'un sieur Reibel, domestique au service de M. Alaux, dentiste.

Au cours de cette opération j'ai été amené à reproduire des empreintes de doigts assez apparentes sur un carreau d'une vitrine du salon de M. Alaux.

Les empreintes dont il s'agit pouvaient avoir été laissées soit par l'assassin présumé, soit par sa victime, soit enfin par une personne quelconque avant pénétré dans le salon de M. Alaux. Dans l'impossibilité matérielle de vérifier la dernière hypothèse je n'avais à m'occuper que des deux premières, ce qui m'a permis tout d'abord de constater que les empreintes inconnues n'avaient aucune analogie avec celle de la victime. Dès lors, les recherches se trouvaient limitées aux répertoires anthropométriques. Effectuées avec le plus grand soin, *elles ont fait découvrir une fiche concernant un nommé Scheffer, Henri Léon, âgé de vingt-six ans,* mesuré le 9 mars dernier comme inculpé de vol et abus de confiance, et dont les empreintes digitales concordent, d'une manière frappante, avec celles relevées sur le lieu du crime.

Afin d'en faciliter la comparaison, j'ai fait aggrandir ces documents à une échelle supérieure de 4 fois à la grandeur naturelle et le rapprochement des épreuves apparaît alors avec la plus grande netteté.

Ci-joint une reproduction des pièces mentionnées au présent rapport.

L'examen des pièces sus-énoncées fait ressortir les constatations suivantes:

Similitude caractéristique du dessin central de chaque empreinte, soit:

1. Pour le Pouce, lacets à direction oblique à droite comprenant 12 sillons entre le point central et le triangle d'intersection.

2. Pour l'Index, lacets à direction oblique à droite comprenant 8 sillons entre le point central et le triangle d'intersection.

3. Pour le Médius, sillons en forme d'arcs superposés avec, au centre de l'empreinte, un seul lacet oblique à droite renfermant un sillon central.

4. Pour l'Annulaire, le centre du dessin est formé d'un point enfermé dans un cercle—à remarquer une légère solution de continuité dans la partie supérieure gauche du cercle—Une spirale entoure ensuite le cercle en commençant par le côté inférieur gauche et finissant, après une triple révolution, sur le côté supérieur gauche. D'autres sillons ou fragments de sillons se greffent sur les côtés de la spirale et la forme générale de l'empreinte se continue en arcs superposés.

A côté de cette similitude de dessins, j'ai également relevé, sur chaque empreinte, un certain nombre de particularités repérées à l'aide de numéros figurant à la fois sur les empreintes relevées sur la vitrine du salon de M. Alaux et sur celles qui existent sur la fiche du nommé, Scheffer, Henri Léon, retrouvée dans les répertoires anthropométriques.

En voici la nomenclature:

No. 1. Sillon bifurqué.
   2. Arrêt du sillon central.
   3. Echancrure formée par un fragment de sillon se greffant sur la partie supérieure gauche du 4e sillon.
1. Pouce. 4. Arrêt du 10e sillon.
   5. Arrêt de sillon.
   6. Sillon bifurqué.
   7. Arrêt du 9e sillon.
   8. Arrêt de sillon.
   9. Arrêt de sillon.
  10. Bifurcation produite par la réunion des 7e et 8e sillons.
  11. Arrêt de sillon.
  12. Arrêt de sillon.

2. Index.

No. 1. Trace de cicatrice située sur le haut de l'empreinte.
   2. Arrêt du sillon central formant boucle.
   3. Crochet formé par la base et le côté gauche du triangle intersection.
   4. Sillon bifurqué.

3. Médius.

No. 1. Trace très apparente de cicatrice située sur le côté gauche de l'empreinte.
   2. Lacet central légèrement échancré dans sa partie supérieure gauche et fragment de sillon se greffant sur la partie supérieure droite.
   3. Sillon bifurqué.
   4. Arrêt de sillon.

4. Annulaire.

No. 1. Arrêt de sillon.
   2. Sillon bifurqué.
   3. Arrêt de sillon.
   4. Sillon bifurqué.
   5. Arrêt externe de la spirale centrale.
   6. Arrêt interne de la spirale centrale.

Conclusions

Il appert que les empreintes digitales photographiées par nous sur la vitre brisée dans un des salons de M. Alaux correspondent exactement à celles que le pouce, l'index, le médius, et l'annulaire de la main droite du nommé Scheffer auraient pu occasioner.

La position respective des traces de doigts imprimées sur les deux faces opposées de cette vitre, savoir : celle du pouce sur la face *extérieure,* et celles de l'index, du médius et de l'annulaire sur la face *intérieure* de la vitrine fracturée, démontre incontestablement que l'apposition de ces empreintes a été faite après le bris de la susdite vitre.

Le Chef du Service de l'Identité Judiciaire,

ALPHONSE BERTILLON

APPENDIX IV

THE PHOTOGRAPH OF THE PRINCE

2, Rue Rude,
Avenue du Bois de Boulogne,
Paris

le 15 mai 1912

MONSIEUR,

Je suis chargé par le Prince de Galles de vous envoyer une photographie comme petit souvenir de la visite intéressante que son Altesse Royale a faite hier à l'admirable service que vous avez organisé.

Veuillez agréer, Monsieur, l'assurance de ma considération la plus distinguée.

H. HANSELL

18—4—1912 [1]

MONSIEUR,

J'ai l'honneur de vous accuser réception de la photographie avec autographe que son Altesse Royale le Prince de Galles a bien voulu me faire addresser, par vos soins, en souvenir de sa visite inoubliable.

Je vous serais très obligé, Monsieur, de vouloir bien, à l'occasion, exprimer à son Altesse Royale combien j'ai été à la fois touché et honoré par cet envoi que je vais placer, dans les archives personnelles, à côté de la Médaille que S. M. la Reine Victoria avait bien voulu m'octroyer jadis.

Veuillez agréer, Monsieur, l'assurance de ma très haute considération.

ALPHONSE BERTILLON
Chef du Service de l'Identité Judiciaire
à la Préfecture de Police de Paris

[1] The date, the fourth month, is evidently a clerical error.

APPENDIX V

Photographic Identification in the Tichborne Case

In 1873 Mr Frederick Piercy, a portrait painter, published an interesting book entitled *A Crucial Test in Cases of Disputed Identity*. The author's methods were a rudimentary but striking anticipation of the *portrait parlé* which Bertillon was to develop a few years later. Identification points relied upon by Mr Piercy were the orientation of the eyes, the form and design of the ears, and the form and size of the central groove which joins the nose and upper lip. These comparisons showed that, whereas the eyes of Roger Tichborne had a slightly upward slant, those of the claimant, Arthur Orton, slanted downward. The ears showed a striking difference in both size and shape. Those of Tichborne were about thirty per cent smaller than those of the claimant. The Tichborne ear had an adhering lobe; that of the claimant was pendulous. They differed also greatly in design, since the Tichborne ear was angular at the summit, but that of the claimant rounded. The groove between nose and upper lip was again much wider in the case of the Tichborne photograph.

Had it been possible to apply the more detailed analysis which Bertillon's work made possible, and which was, in fact, applied by Professor Bischoff in the Tchaikovsky Case, the Tichborne/Orton photographs might have been shown to be conclusive, as in fact they were for all practical purposes. In the event, the evidence was severely attacked, and it was never—as was the expert evidence in the Tchaikovsky Case—accepted as final in itself.

APPENDIX VI

Bertillon and Ultra-violet Photography

The late Dr Eugène Stockis, formerly the Director of the Laboratories of Technical Police of Liège, Belgium, in a memorial paper to Bertillon pays a particular tribute to his work in the field of technical photography, not only in connexion with the photography of the individual but in connexion with that of documents. He adds that Bertillon studied the applications of ultra-violet rays to document photography.

Dr Stockis kept very closely in touch with Bertillon's work, and his statement is of considerable historical interest. (See Eugène Stockis, *Alphonse Bertillon* (Archives Internationales de Médecine Légale, vol. V, Fascicule 2—Avril 1914, page 6).)

No other allusion to Bertillon's work with ultra-violet rays has been traced elsewhere. But these experiments may well represent the earliest attempts to utilize ultra-violet photography for the examination of documents. Bertillon is well known to have favoured the use of the carbon arc as a source of illumination for certain kinds of photography. The carbon arc is a source of ultra-violet, and it may well be that Bertillon made use of some form of ultra-violet filter experimentally.

The first systematized use of ultra-violet rays for the examination of documents appears to have been developed by the American Military Intelligence during the 1914–18 war for the examination of invisible ink. It was not, however, until about 1923 that ultra-violet photography began to be widely used.

APPENDIX VII

The " Bordereau "

The Dreyfus Case, by Guy Chapman (London, 1955), was not published until after the present book was completed, so that the author had not the advantage of consulting it until after this book was in proof. Professor Chapman's book is an important contribution to the history of the affair.

In a letter to the present author Professor Chapman drew attention to the interesting fact that there is evidence which suggests that the original *bordereau* was examined by other experts besides Gobert and Bertillon. He reaches this conclusion because it was reported that the unusual paper upon which the document was written matched the writing paper used by Esterhazy. It was also stated that this kind of '*pelure*' paper was no longer being manufactured. This would establish (1) that Esterhazy was in possession of, and was accustomed to use, paper of the *bordereau* type, and (2) that, since the manufacture of this type of paper had been discontinued, it is unlikely that it would have been available to anyone else.

If these facts could be accepted without question it should seem to establish the authorship of the *bordereau*. But the evidence is far from being conclusive. It is quite certain that no paper-expert had an opportunity to make a sufficiently detailed examination of the *bordereau* paper to justify a positive opinion. In a case where so much of the expert evidence is suspect it is even less satisfactory than the opinions expressed concerning the handwriting. There is nothing in Bertillon's report or evidence to suggest that the paper had any unusual characteristics. On the contrary, the implication is that it was the type of paper commonly used for foreign correspondence. In the circumstances it seems reasonable to assume that this opinion was one of those rash assertions which were all too frequently made in connexion with the *bordereau*.

REFERENCES

<small>UNPUBLISHED CORRESPONDENCE CONSULTED</small>

Zoé Bertillon to Louis-Adolphe Bertillon, July 1863

Alphonse Bertillon to Jacques Bertillon, August 1863

Louis-Adolphe Bertillon to Jacques Bertillon, July 1865

Zoé Bertillon to Jacques Bertillon, Ussat, July 1865

Alphonse Bertillon to Jacques Bertillon, Institut Rossat, October 1865

Louis-Adolphe Bertillon to Jacques Bertillon, Ussat, July 1865

Alphonse Bertillon to Jacques Bertillon, Ussat, September 1867

Alphonse Bertillon to Jacques Bertillon, Ussat, August 1867

Alphonse Bertillon to Louis-Adolphe Bertillon, Havre, December 1871

Alphonse Bertillon to Jacques Bertillon, Havre, October, November, and December 1871

Louis-Adolphe Bertillon and Georges Bertillon to Alphonse Bertillon, July 1871

Louis-Adolphe Bertillon to Jacques Bertillon, June 1871

Georges Bertillon to Alphonse Bertillon, undated, 1871

Jacques Bertillon to Alphonse Bertillon, June 1871

Alphonse Bertillon to Jacques Bertillon, Havre, June 1871

Jacques Bertillon to Alphonse Bertillon, Paris, June 1871

Louis-Adolphe Bertillon to Jacques Bertillon, Laval, June 1871

Louis-Adolphe Bertillon to Alphonse Bertillon, Le Mans, June 1871

Louis-Adolphe Bertillon to son [?], Le Mans, undated, 1871

Alphonse Bertillon to Jacques Bertillon, London, April 1873

Alphonse Bertillon to Jacques Bertillon, Smethwick, March 1874

Claire de Charnacé to Louis-Adolphe Bertillon, Versailles, July 1874

Alphonse Bertillon to Jacques Bertillon, 7 Arundel Street, Coventry Street, London, W., December 1874

Alphonse Bertillon to Jacques Bertillon, Smethwick, February 1874

Alphonse Bertillon to Louis-Adolphe Bertillon, Smethwick, February 1874

William Grant to Alphonse Bertillon, Smethwick, June 1874
Alphonse Bertillon to Jacques Bertillon, 54 St Mary's Terrace,
Paddington, July 1874
George Wilks to Alphonse Bertillon, Bishops Stortford, January
1875
Alphonse Bertillon to Jacques Bertillon, Roanne, undated, 1875
Alphonse Bertillon to Jacques Bertillon, Roanne, February 1875

BOOKS AND PAMPHLETS

Achille, L., *Le Service Anthropométrique de M. Bertillon*
(*Rapport sur le Budget de la Préfecture de Police*) (1909).
Almandos, Luis, *Bertillon et Vucetich* (La Plata, 1928).
Almandos, Luis, *Dactiloscopía Argentina* (La Plata, 1909).
Almandos, Luis, *Documentación del Museo Vucetich* (La Plata,
1928).
Bertillon, A., *L'Anthropométrie Judiciaire à Paris en 1889* (Paris
et Lyon, 1890).
Bertillon, A., *Le Classement Phonétique* (Paris, 1896).
Bertillon, A., *La Couleur de l'Iris* (*Rev. Sci.*, July 1885).
Bertillon, A., *Les Empreintes Digitales* (*Arch. de Lacassagne*, 15
jan., 1912).
Bertillon, A., *Identification Anthropométrique* (*Ann. de Démo-
graphie*, 1882).
Bertillon, A., *Instructions Signalétiques* (Melun, 1893).
Bertillon, A., *Notice sur les Empreintes Digitales* (Service de
l'Identité Judiciaire, 1903).
Bertillon, A., *Notice sur le Fonctionnement du Service d'Identifi-
cation* (*Annuaire Statistique de la Ville de Paris*, 1887).
Bertillon, A., *Les Proportions du Corps Humain* (*Rev. Sci.*, 1889).
Bertillon, A., *La Comparaison des Ecritures* (*Rev. Sci.*, 1898).
Bertillon, A., *La Photographie Judiciaire* (Paris, 1890).
Bertillon, A., *Les Races Sauvages* (Paris, 1882).
Bertillon, A., *Service des Signalements* (Lyon, 1888).
Bertillon, J., *Cours Elémentaire de Statistique Administrative*
(Paris, 1896).
Bertillon, J., *La Dépopulation de la France* (Paris, 1911).
Bertillon, J., *La Statistique Humaine de la France* (Paris, 1885).
Bertillon, L.-A., *De quelques Eléments de l'Hygiéne* (Thèse de
Paris, 1852).
Bertillon, L.-A., *La Démographie Figurée de la France* (Paris,
1874).
Bertillon, L.-A., *Dictionnaire des Sciences Anthropologiques*
(Paris, 1883).

Bertillon, Suzanne, *Vie d'Alphonse Bertillon* (Paris, 1940).

Burke's Peerage[1] (London, 1955).

Chapel, C. E., *Fingerprinting* (London, 1946).

Cherrill, F. R., *The Fingerprint System at Scotland Yard* (London, 1954).

Faulds, Henry, *Dactylography* (Halifax, 1912).

Faulds, Henry, *Guide to Fingerprint Identification* (Hanley, 1905).

Faulds, Henry, *The Hidden Hand* (pamphlet) (Hanley, 1917).

Ferrer, R. V., *Manuel de Identificación*.

Forgeot, R., *Les Empreintes Digitales étudiées au point de vue Médico-judiciaire* (Lyon, 1891).

Frecon, A., *Les Empreintes en général* (Thèse de Lyon, 1889).

Galton, F., *Enquiries into Human Faculty* (London, 1928).

Galton, F., *Fingerprints* (London, 1892).

Galton, F., *Memories of My Life* (London, 1908).

Gilliard, P., and Switch, C., *La Fausse Anastasie* (Paris, 1929).

Goddefroy, E., *Manuel Elémentaire de Police Technique* (Bruxelles, 1922).

Griffiths, A., *Mysteries of Police and Crime* (London, 1901, etc.).

Gross, Hanns, *Criminal Investigation* (London, 1949).

Heindl, R., *Daktyloscopie* (Berlin, 1927).

Henry, Edward, *Classification and Uses of Fingerprints* (London, 1900).

Herschel, W. J., *The Origin of Fingerprinting* (London, 1916).

Lacassagne, A., *La Signification du Tatouage* (*Arch. de Lacassagne*, 1912).

Lacassagne, A., and Locard, E., *Alphonse Bertillon* (Lyon, 1914).

Locard, Ed., *Manuel de Technique Policière* (Paris, 1923).

Locard, Ed., *L'Enquête Criminelle et les Méthodes Scientifiques* (Paris, 1920).

Locard, Ed., *Traité de Criminalistique* (7 vols.) (Lyon, 1931–40).

Maugham, Frederic Herbert, Viscount, *The Tichborne Case* (London, 1936).

Mitchell, C. A., *The Expert Witness* (Cambridge, 1923).

Mitchell, C. A., *Science and the Criminal* (London, 1911).

Niceforo, A., *La Police et l'Enquête Judiciaire Scientifiques* (Paris, 1907).

Ottolenghi, S., *Trattato de Polizia Scientifica* (Rome, 1911).

Quételet, A., *Anthropométrie, ou Mesure des Différentes Facultés de l'Homme* (Bruxelles, 1870).

[1] The author is indebted to Mr Peter Townend, assistant editor of *Burke's Peerage*, who supplied some interesting details concerning the Hanbury family.

Reiss, R. A., *Manuel de Police Scientifique* (Lausanne, 1911).
Reiss, R. A., *Le Portrait Parlé* (Paris, 1905).
Rhodes, H. T. F., *Forensic Chemistry* (London, 1947).
Rhodes, H. T. F. (editor), *In the Tracks of Crime* (London, 1952).
Stockis, Eugène, *Alphonse Bertillon* (Arch. Inter. de Med. Leg.) (Liège, 1914).
Vucetich, J., *Historia sintética de la Identificación: Revista de Identificación.* (Posthumous.) (Jul.–Agos., 1930).
Wilder, H. H., and Wentworth, B., *Personal Identification* (Boston, 1918).

The Dreyfus Case

Anonymous, *Le Bordereau: Etude des Dépositions de M. Bertillon et du Capitaine Valério* (Paris, 1904).
Anonymous, *La Clé de l'Affaire Dreyfus* (Paris, 1899).
Biez, J. de, *Le Solécisme du Bordereau et les Lettres de Dreyfus* (Paris, 1898).
Blum, Léon, *Souvenirs sur l'Affaire* [*Dreyfus*] (Paris, 1935).
Bonnamour, G., *La Déposition de M. Bertillon devant la Cour de Cassation* (Paris, 1899).
Bonnamour, G., *Le Procès Dreyfus* (Paris, 1899).
Chapman, Guy, *The Dreyfus Case* (London, 1955). (This is a valuable reassessment of the evidence.)
Conybeare, F. C., *The Dreyfus Case* (London, 1898).
Cornély, J., *Notes sur l'Affaire Dreyfus* (Paris, 1899).
Crépieux-Jamin, J., *L'Expertise en Ecritures et les Leçons de l'Affaire Dreyfus* (Paris, 1907).
Dubreuil, R., *L'Affaire Dreyfus devant la Cour de Cassation* (Paris, 1899).
Foucault, A., *Un Nouvel Aspect de l'Affaire Dreyfus* (Paris, 1938).
Guyot, Y., *Affaire Dreyfus: Analyse de l'Enquête* (Paris, 1899).
Kohler, Max J., *Some New Light on the Dreyfus Case* (Vienna, 1929).
Latigney, G. de, *L'Affaire Dreyfus: Le Redan de M. Bertillon.*
Lazare, B., *Une Erreur Judiciaire* (Paris, 1897).
Locard, Ed., *L'Affaire Dreyfus* (Lyon, 1937).
Marie, P., *Le Petit Bleu* (Paris, 1899).
Molé, P., *Exposé Impartial de l'Affaire Dreyfus* (Paris, 1899).
Reinach, J., *Histoire de l'Affaire Dreyfus* (Paris, 1901–11).
Schwartzkoppen, M. von, *The Truth about Dreyfus* (London, 1931).
Testis, J., *La Trahison Esterhazy et Schwartzkoppen* (Paris, 1898).
Vanex, J., *Dossier de l'Affaire Dreyfus* (Paris, 1898).

INDEX